BENMILLER
then and now

BENMILLER
then and now

Joanne Ivey

ISBN 0-9694241-0-8

Printed and bound in Canada by D.W. Friesen & Sons Ltd.,
Altona, Manitoba

Reprinted 1995

COVER PHOTOS
Front: The Woollen Mill in winter, 1976. (Photo: Integrated
Graphics)
Back: Benmiller, c.1900. (Photo: Huron County Museum)

ACKNOWLEDGEMENTS

First I should like to thank the present management and owners of Benmiller Inn for their cooperation and support in this venture. My thanks also to the Huron County Museum in Goderich for searching out and allowing me to photograph their early photos of Benmiller, and to Dorothy Fisher and Norman Durst for providing family information and photos.

Thanks as well to Margaret Garbarino and James Lafer of Detroit, Michigan, for sending me their fine photos of the Gledhills and Ray Moore at work in the Woollen Mill; to Beulah Long for allowing me to pore over her scrap books; to Ann Ryder from British Columbia, niece of Willa and Verne Gledhill, for her information about the family and her reminiscences of her uncles at work in the mill; to Ray Kennedy for answering my many questions about the operation of the generator room, the solar heating and so on; and special thanks to Brad Vanstone for clueing me in when my memory failed me and for his very pertinent suggestions regarding the text.

Thanks to my family and friends for their assistance and support, with special mention to Clare for her expert advice and word processor. Finally, thanks to Robin Brass, editor in chief, layout artist and general factotum, for guiding me around the many pitfalls of producing a book.

JOANNE IVEY

To Peter

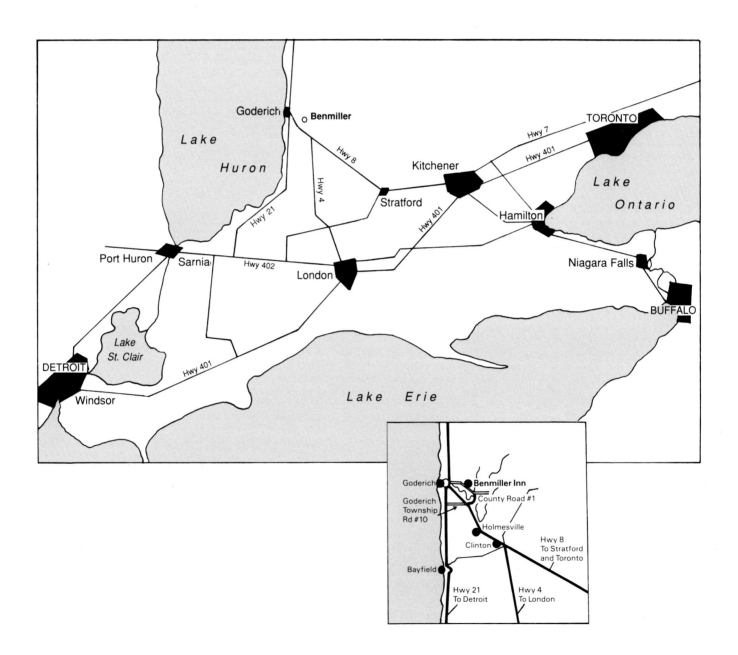

Contents

Preface   9

Old Benmiller   11

The Woollen Mill   35

The River Mill   75

Adding Houses   105

Cherrydale   123

Looking Back   133

1 Joseph Guisbuch, tanner
2 Jacob Hediger, painter
3 Gotfried Maedal
4 Thomas Good, stone lime kiln
5 Cheese factory
6 Rodney Adams, cradle maker
7 Pfrimmer, miller
8 Benmiller Hotel
9 William Robertson, blacksmith
10 John Stewart, fruit grower
11 Andrew Heddle, carpenter
12 Frederic Larmey, tailor
13 Frederic Speight, weaver
14 Thomas Kerr, shoemaker
15 Samuel Walker, teacher
16 Benmiller School
17 Woollen Mill
18 James Long, farmer
19 Benmiller General Store
20 James Cottle, blacksmith
21 Joshua Moore, shoemaker
22 Gledhill
23 Gledhill
24 Wagon Shop
25 Grist Mill
26 Pfrimmer
27 Gledhill

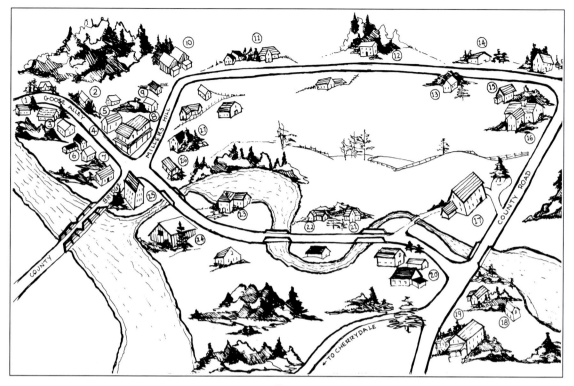

Benmiller *c*.1900

1 Jack McLaren
2 Abandoned house of Gotfried Maedal
3 Mill House – Benmiller Inn
4 River Mill – Benmiller Inn
5 Swimming pool – Benmiller Inn
6 Tennis courts – Benmiller Inn
7 Barn – Benmiller Inn
8 Workshop – Benmiller Inn
9 Log house – Upper Lands West, Benmiller Estates
10 Schoolhouse – Canadian Legion
11 Woollen Mill – Benmiller Inn
12 General Store
13 Forge
14 Manager's house – Benmiller Inn
15 Gledhill House – Benmiller Inn

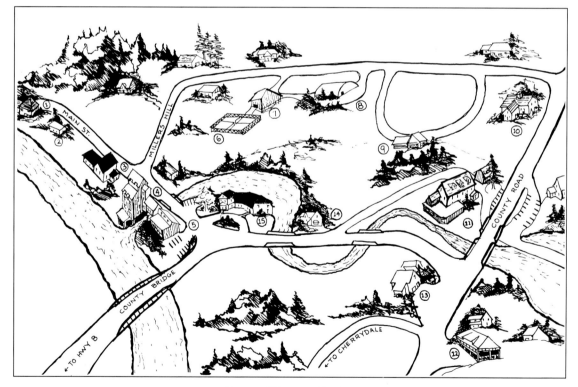

Benmiller *c*.1980

Preface

SPRINGS determined the location of the earliest settlers in Huron County. They looked for flowing streams as travellers looked for an oasis in the desert.

The village of Benmiller is situated on the Maitland River about seven miles east of Goderich. It nestles in a hollow beside a fast-flowing stream that winds its way through the hamlet, creating a setting of lovely tranquility. This stream, known as Sharpe's Creek, was named after a runaway slave who was Benmiller's first inhabitant. He lived in a squatter's hut on its bank. The village was originally known as Colborne Mills because of its location in the Township of Colborne and because of the mills that sprang up along the stream. At one time there were three mills powered by this creek.

Later the name of the village was changed to Benmiller, after one of its first settlers. Benjamin Miller sat on the first township council, and the bridge across the Maitland River where Sharpe's Creek joined it was always referred to by council as Ben Miller's bridge. Years after Ben's death, the name was finally changed.

Whenever I visited this beautiful little village as a child, I was aware of its sense of history. Whether this feeling came from the mills themselves which were still operating as they had for almost 100 years, or whether it was because of the remoteness of the village, I am not sure. I only know that when I went to Benmiller with my family I always had the feeling that the twentieth century had passed it by. It is for this reason that I begin my story with a short history of the village, its earliest settlers, its rise and decline. Without knowing what went before it is difficult for the reader to understand what my brother Peter and I struggled so hard to maintain—namely, this very sense of history.

JOANNE IVEY

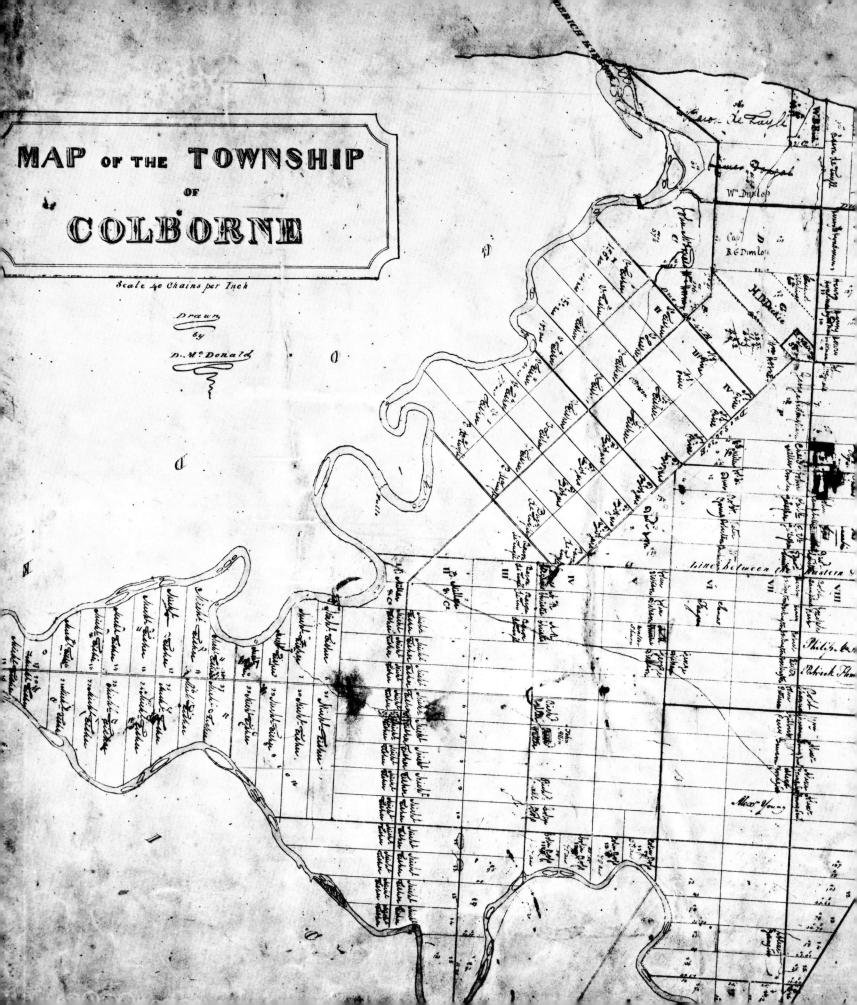

Old Benmiller

A S FAR BACK as historians can trace, the Indians who lived in the Huron County area called themselves Attawandarons. French explorers and missionaries called them Neutrals, for when they first came to know this tribe they were amazed to find that the Indians seemed able to live in peace with their warlike neighbours to the north, the Hurons, and their equally warlike neighbours to the south, the Iroquois. The reason was that they controlled the supply of flint found at Kettle Point on the shores of Lake Huron. Without flint for arrow and spear heads the Iroquois could not cope with the Hurons nor the Hurons with the Iroquois.

The Neutrals were well advanced in growing beans, tobacco, corn, squash and other vegetables. An early seventeenth-century French missionary called them "physically the finest body of men that I have ever seen anywhere." These then were the people encountered by the first white man to come to Huron County. He was Etienne Brulé, a young adventurer who had come with Champlain on his fifth voy-

age to New France in 1608. He was just sixteen, fresh from a small farm in France. He quickly proved adept at mastering the various Indian dialects and eventually became the foremost interpreter of his time. He decided he wanted to spend the rest of his life among the Huron Indians, but the Indians at first resisted, for they were sure they would be blamed if anything should happen to the "young white." Finally it was agreed that Champlain would exchange Brulé for a young Huron brave called Savignon, who would accompany him back to France. Twenty-five years later, because of his unscrupulous behaviour with the Indian maidens, Brulé was quartered and eaten by the braves of the Bear tribe of the Hurons.

On a later voyage, in 1615, Champlain is said to have worked his way through the inland waterway up along the eastern shore of Lake Huron and to have camped both on his way up and back on the spot where Goderich now stands.

It was 1626 before the next white man ventured into Neutral territory. He was a Récollet missionary called Father d'Aillan, who set out alone with nothing more than a staff and a pack on his back. As he went deeper into the territory he was forced by the Neutral Indians to flee for his life back to the Huron mission stations on Georgian Bay.

By 1640 the Jesuits, who had taken over from the Récollets, were well established throughout the Georgian Bay area. In that year, Fathers Brébeuf and

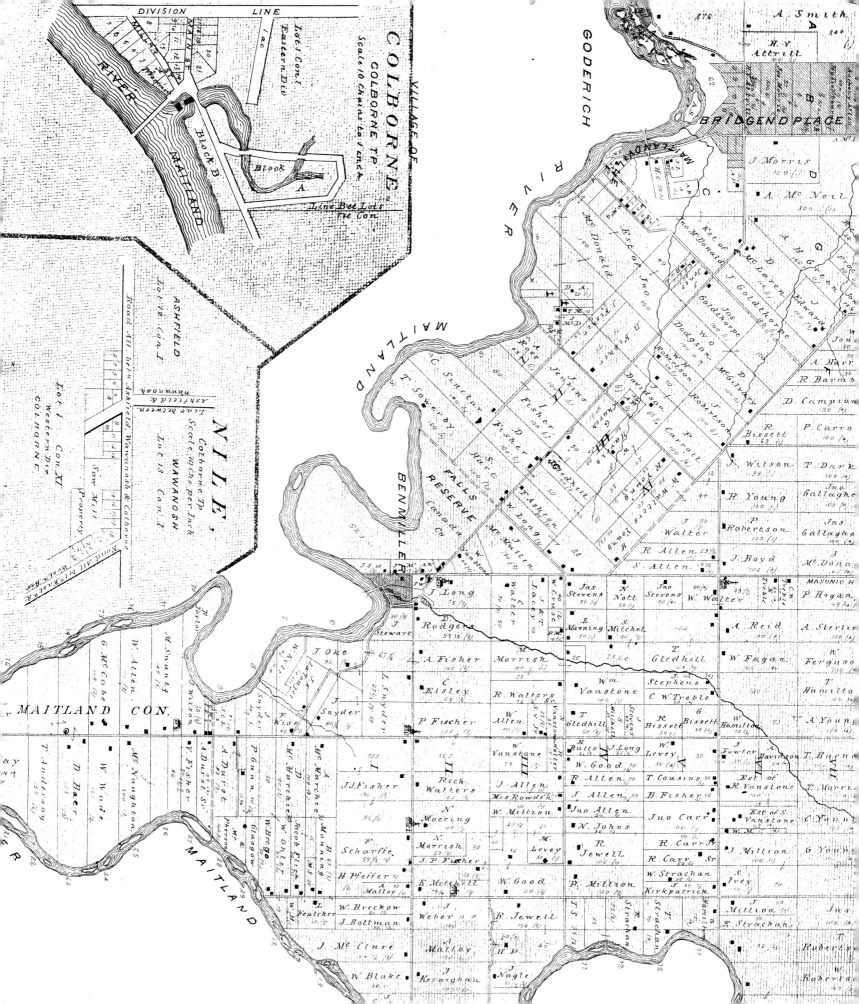

Chaumonot set out once more to try to penetrate the Neutral's territory, but again they were driven back. During their short stay, however, Brébeuf gathered enough material for the first dictionary of the Neutral dialect.

Over the years the feud between the Hurons and the Iroquois grew in ferocity. It was a battle for supremacy in the fur trade with the white man. By 1648 the Iroquois, spurred on by hatred of the French, who had sworn to protect the Hurons, were ready to launch an all-out attack. By the time they had finished, the Hurons had been virtually eliminated and the French mission settlements had been razed.

All through this the Neutrals maintained their impartiality. They began to trade with the white man and built a reputation for their fine pelts. The fur-hungry Iroquois, with the heat of victory upon them, turned on the Neutrals, and by the fall of 1650 the once-prosperous Attawandarons had been massacred to extinction.

For almost 200 years the eastern shore of Lake Huron was the casual hunting ground of the Chippewa and Mohawk bands of the Iroquois nation. (One of their burial grounds was in the Falls Conservation Area adjacent to the village of Benmiller.) During this time, Canada passed from the hands of the French to the British, but while settlement went ahead elsewhere, southwestern Ontario was left untouched because of its relative inaccessibility. Explorers, traders and settlers flowed west both to the south and the north of this area but the Huron district was left alone.

The Canada Company

The first obstacle to access was overcome when a military road was built from Lake Simcoe to Georgian Bay during the War of 1812, to set up a dockyard at Penetanguishene so that warships could sail down Lake Huron and into Lake Erie. The man chosen to build the road was an army doctor called William "Tiger" Dunlop, one of the most eccentric personages of Canadian history, who was later to play a key role in the development of the Goderich area.

In 1825 the government of Upper Canada in Toronto (then York), pressured by demand for land by incoming settlers, became interested in the eastern shores of Lake Huron. In April of that year the chief of the Chippewa Indians signed an agreement selling the Crown 2,200,000 acres. In payment 400 members of the chief's tribe and their descendants were to receive £1,100 per annum for ever.

Shortly before this, in 1824, a Scottish dreamer, novelist, journalist and traveller named John Galt had formed the Canada Company. This Ayrshire-born visionary believed that the only salvation for his oppressed countrymen was emigration and he persuaded Scottish and English capitalists to invest in land in Canada. His plan was to promote development by means of a company instead of involving the government. He would then be able to provide good cheap land for the thousands of poverty-stricken crofters who had attracted his sympathy. Settlers were to be transported to colonies and placed on the land at a price stipulated in advance and given assistance during the difficult transition period. Help was to be given to them with such public conveniences as roads, bridges, schools and churches, and the stockholders were to receive a fair profit.

Galt's company was incorporated in 1824 and properly organized in 1825. Certain specified Crown lands and clergy reserves were to be made available to the company at a price set by a commission headed by Galt, who would go to Upper Canada to assess the land. He had scarcely returned to England when he was told that Bishop Strachan in York had forbidden the sale of the clergy reserves. It was finally resolved

FACING PAGE
Section of map from page 9 of the 1879 Huron County Atlas, including an inset of "Colborne," which on the main map is labelled Benmiller.

in May of 1826 that the British government would sell to the company just over a million acres of the territory recently purchased from the Chippewa Indians. In all the Canada Company now had 2,484,413 acres of land. The land purchased from the Indians was known as the Huron Tract and included Colborne Township, where the village of Benmiller now stands. The price paid was about 90 cents per acre. This land was later sold to the settlers at $1.50 to $2.50 per acre, a fair enough price for all concerned. By the spring of 1827 all arrangements were completed in London and Galt was appointed to return to Upper Canada to superintend the activities of the company.

He set up his headquarters in Guelph and hired Tiger Dunlop to head a survey party to blaze a trail to the shores of Lake Huron. The party included another able Scot by the name of John McDonald who later did the surveying of the Goderich area. Galt meanwhile took the road to Penetanguishene and sailed down the Huron shore to meet Dunlop's party. When he came to the spot where Goderich now stands, Galt wrote: "We saw far off by our telescope, a small clearing in the forest and on the brow of a rising ground a cottage delightfully situated…. About an hour after having crossed the river's bar of eight feet, we came to a beautiful anchorage of fourteen feet of water in an uncommonly pleasant small basin…. Here we landed, and cheerfully spent the night in the log cottage which the Doctor had raised."

Tiger Dunlop became the Canada Company's Warden of the Woods and Forests, and through his literary gifts and Galt's, in pamphlets and newspaper articles circulated back home, settlers were attracted to the Huron Tract. In 1828 the Canada Company tried to interest several experienced settlers from York (Toronto) in the Huron Tract. The company provided a schooner to take them to Niagara-on-the-Lake. From there they travelled overland by stage coach to Chippewa, where they boarded another boat for the voyage through Lake Erie and into Lake Huron. Michael Fisher and his brother Valentine, known as Feltie, were among these settlers. Their father, Jacob, was of German ancestry and had come from Pennsylvania to Upper Canada to settle in Vaughan Township, York County, in 1780. Michael, born in 1786, married Susannah Holly and moved to Waterloo, where he operated a chopping mill. Later he moved back to York, where he had a large farm on Yonge Street.

Michael was experienced in the ways of the pioneer and, when he arrived in Goderich, immediately set about exploring the territory. Legend has it that he took a rowboat up the Maitland River (known to the Indians as the Minnesetung) until he came to a large spring and was so impressed with the site's possibilities that he purchased from the Canada Company a block of 5,465 acres adjacent to the present-day village of Benmiller. He paid $10,000, a considerable sum for a farmer in those days. His brother, Valentine, at the same time acquired a large tract along the Maitland River west of the Falls Conservation Area extending almost to the present-day village of Saltford. The deeds were registered in the Huron County Registry Office and signed by Thomas Mercer Jones, who succeeded Galt as commissioner of the Canada Company.

On his holding Michael Fisher built a saw mill and log shanty. In 1831 he built a log cabin and made his first clearing of the land. This clearing became a cherry orchard. In 1834 he brought a staff of builders and most of the materials from York to construct a stone dwelling to house his wife, seven sons and three daughters. One early settler upon arriving in the area asked who his neighbour might be. The answer was, "If you meet someone on the road, just say 'Good day, Mr. Fisher,' and you will probably be right."

Michael Fisher's stone house, now known as Cherrydale, still stands virtually intact, a monument to the early craftsmen who built it. In 1844 he traded Cherrydale and two other farms he owned nearby to Henry Martin for a chopping mill, flour mill, saw mill

In 1877 Jesse Gledhill built the present two-storey cast lime building. The lime came from

In Jesse's time the power for the mill (right) came from an upright, exposed, paddle-type wheel at the end of a wooden flume that directed the tail waters from Sharpe's Creek. This print was used on the letterhead of our first notepaper, which in turn had been used by the Gledhills for the woollen mill.

In 1930 the power source was modernized. The wheel was replaced by a 50-horsepower turbine. A steel pipe carried water from the upper dam. (Photo taken by Ray Moore and lent by his daughter, Dorothy Fisher)

and forty acres of land back in Vaughan Township. He still had enough land left to leave his sons 300 acres each. Michael Fisher's brother, Feltie, stayed on in Goderich to become a local character. He and his English wife ran a log inn near the harbour that became a favourite place for political meetings.

SETTLEMENT BEGINS

A year or two after Michael Fisher arrived, Benjamin Miller came with his brothers, Daniel and Joseph. Born in Upper Canada of English origin, Benjamin was what today might be called a developer. By his many shrewd purchases, the holdings of the Benjamin Miller and Company became considerable, though it is difficult to determine their full extent as there was no inventory attached to his will when he died in 1858. The earliest Canada Company map of Colborne Township, dated 1831, when the area was surveyed, shows that most of the key lands in the village that now bears his name were owned by Ben Miller. We know that in September 1844, when acquiring title to a piece of land in Goderich, Ben was listed as an innkeeper of that town. The deed for the land where Miller's hotel was built on Lot 1, Concession 1, Colborne eastern division (now part of the village of Benmiller), dated 1848, described him as a yeoman of the Township of Colborne. By now, the B. Miller and Co. had built the first grist mill and saw mill on Sharpe's Creek and had acquired a large parcel of land up on the flats to the west, overlooking the village, which Joseph operated as a farm.

It is easy to see why a shrewd developer in the mid-nineteenth century would consider the land along Sharpe's Creek a bargain, though Ben had to pay £136 for five acres, which was considerably more than the going rate for farm land in the area. The headwaters of the creek lie in the Saratoga Swamp, which acts as a reservoir, ensuring a continuous water flow even in dry weather, making the creek ideal for powering mills.

Soon the B. Miller and Co. began to sell small parcels of land. One of the first was an acre to Sinclair Meiklejohn, a blacksmith. It must have been a key piece of property, for even to this day it is said that all surveying started from Meiklejohn's acre.

In 1852 Ben Miller sold land to William and Thomas Logan, who built the first woollen mill, a frame building a short distance up the creek from the grist mill where the Gledhill House now is. In 1857, Thomas Gledhill bought the woollen mill from Thomas Logan. The Gledhills had been in the woollen business in Leeds, England, before emigrating to America. Thomas was born in Yorkshire, as was his wife, Mary. They married in 1832 at Leeds and emigrated to New York State in the summer of 1842 with four children, Henry, John, Jesse (four years old) and Edwin. A son, Thomas, was born to them there. The family later moved to Campbellville, near Guelph, and it was while they were there that Thomas heard of a mill for sale in Colborne Mills, as Benmiller was then known. Thomas and his son Jesse journeyed on foot along the Huron Road, built by Dunlop some twenty-five years earlier through Stratford and Mitchell, to look the prospect over. They liked what they saw and arranged to move there. In the 1861 census, Thomas was listed as a weaver and woollen manufacturer. He had six employees and that year produced 2,000 yards of fulled cloth. He died later that same year and left the business to his five sons. Jesse Gledhill bought out his brothers and successfully operated the mill until it was destroyed by fire in 1877.

Jesse then built the present two-storey, cast lime building further up the creek. The lime came from a stone lime kiln situated by the river near the grist mill. Cast lime was the forerunner of modern poured concrete and the woollen mill was one of the first buildings of its kind. The footings were on hardpan. Moulds were built of wood about one foot high and the concrete was poured layer by layer. The outside dimensions were 40 by 70 feet. At the time it was said

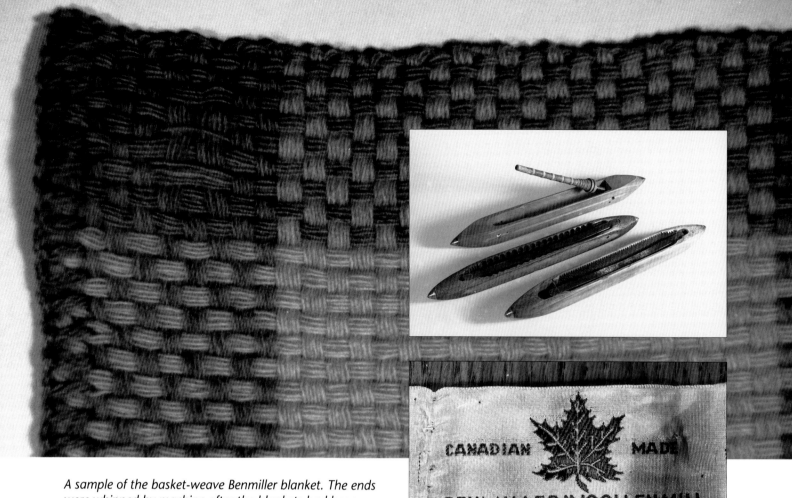

A sample of the basket-weave Benmiller blanket. The ends were whipped by machine after the blankets had been washed and stretched. The inset photos show three kinds of shuttles used on the looms and an example of the label that went on each blanket. (Photos: Bluewater Photography)

that the building could not withstand the constant vibration of the heavy machinery, but it still stands over 100 years later, as sturdy as ever.

The building was simple with no basement. There were two floors for machinery and an attic for drying the wool and blankets in the winter. Behind the mill were 200 feet of wood and concrete racks used for drying and stretching the blankets in fair weather. The concrete posts still stand, supporting lamps that light the way into the Inn at night. In Jesse's time the mill's power came from an upright water wheel beside Sharpe's Creek. In 1930 the power source was completely modernized. The wheel was replaced with a 50-horsepower turbine. A steel pipe 4 feet in diame-

ter and more than 40 feet long carried water from the upper dam and connected with a similar vertical pipe from the penstock or sluice gate that opened to let the water through to drive the turbine. At the creek side of the mill was a shed that housed the turbine as well as large concrete vats where the dyeing of the wool took place. Normally the mill was powered entirely by water from Sharpe's Creek but in times of drought a steam engine took over. Its boiler also supplied all the heat for the building in the winter months. Before we bought the building the engine was driven out of the mill under its own steam and sold.

In just under 100 years of operation only normal maintenance was required on the building. Other machinery was replaced over the years, but the carding machine was the original one brought to Benmiller by ox team from Stratford when Jesse built the mill. With the new equipment, production was expanded to include ordinary brushed wool blankets, car rugs and coolers for horses, as well as the famous basket-weave Benmiller blankets in green, blue or soft rose. The ends of the blankets were whipped by machine after they had been washed, dried and stretched. A Goderich fabric merchant who bought and sold the Benmiller blankets for forty years said, "If there was the odd piece of burr in it, you knew it was a genuine Benmiller blanket. They didn't need a label."

In 1915 Ward Gledhill took over the operation of the mill from his father, Jesse. In the same year Ward's son Verne was decorated in France with the Distinguished Conduct Medal for bravery. In 1920 Ward and his two sons, Verne and Clyde, formed a partnership.

Before Jesse Gledhill died in 1919, he built the small park area near the front entrance to the mill with a fountain and places to sit around it. In his day, family and friends would gather in the summer for relaxation or picnics. There was always a cold drink of spring water available. The fountain and seats have been retained much as they were, though the surrounding area has been laid with brick and the inside of the fountain has been painted.

There is a story about Ward Gledhill that local people like to tell. In the early years of World War II someone kept breaking into the mill and stealing 400-pound burlap bales of fleece. Ward decided to take the law into his own hands. He lay in wait for several nights with a large gun at his side. When the unsuspecting thief finally appeared, Ward took aim and fired. It turned out to be a competitor from a neigh-

Large piles of wool in the background wait to be processed. (Photo courtesy of Dorothy Fisher)

Jesse Gledhill and family. Left to right: Jesse's daughter Florence, his wife, Sarah Jane Vanstone Gledhill, his son Ward, his granddaughter Gertrude, and Jesse. (Photo courtesy of Dorothy Fisher)

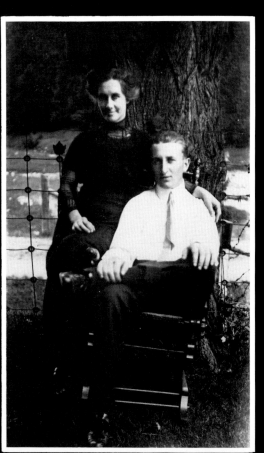

This photo of Ward Gledhill hangs in Gledhill House.

(Above) Jesse Gledhill at age 81. (Photo: Huron County Museum)

(Left) Verne Gledhill with his Aunt Florence Gledhill. (Photo courtesy of Dorothy Fisher)

bouring village and a court case followed. I do not know who was charged with what but the culprit recuperated and Ward was treated with the utmost respect from then on. It was the last robbery at the woollen mill.

Until his death in 1943 Ward operated the mill with the help of Verne and Clyde, and his nephew, Ray Moore. Ward's wife, Charlotte Moore, was Ray's aunt. At its peak the mill employed as many as ten people but in later years, after Ward's death, it was operated by just the three men. During World War II it was difficult to find experienced help and the government cut the wool ration to 40 per cent of the required supply. In the end the mill was producing only the basket-weave blankets.

The entire operation, from washing the fleece, to carding, dyeing, spinning, weaving and marketing was completed on the premises. Fleeces were bought through the Canadian Wool Growers Cooperative. They arrived in huge burlap bags weighing 400 to 500 pounds. The wool had to be washed and cleaned of burdock and other debris, then it went into the carding machine. During the war, Verne and Clyde's niece, Ann (daughter of their only sister, Gertrude), spent her summers with her grandparents, the senior Gledhills, in the old Gledhill house. She passed much of the time at the mill watching her uncles at work. She writes: "The washed fleece was oiled before it went through the picker prior to being carded. This kept the dust down and the fibres moist during processing. Everything, including the mill floor, was covered with many layers of grease. Some fleece was dyed in a huge vat and I was warned to keep away from the edge as it was an acid bath to make the colours fast. This fleece was dried in the attic of the mill. It was spread out on the floor in colour groups. The fleece didn't take long to dry in the extreme temperatures that developed on a sunny day near the roof of the mill. The dyed fleece was mixed with white fleece to develop the final coloured yarn...."

"I wanted to help in all stages of the wool preparation but probably was more of a nuisance as it wasn't very safe for children. The belts and wheels were everywhere as they turned the machines. As I remember, Verne operated the upstairs machinery, including the 'mule' or spinner. That machine twisted the thick ropes of the carded wool into fine single-ply threads. It was a magnificent piece of machinery that went from wall to wall. I was fascinated with its progress along its tracks on the floor, always expecting something to break as it stretched and twisted the fibres to maximum before winding the thread on to the bobbins. Occasionally a thread did break and Verne would see it and repair the thread...."

Clyde Gledhill and Ray Moore worked the broad looms on the ground floor that wove the yarn into blanket cloth. After the yardage was washed, it took all three men to hang it on the drying and stretching racks in the attic or outside. It was hard work—ten hours a day, six days a week. In 1964 the hard work took its toll. Verne suffered a heart attack and the looms shut down for the last time. Clyde died two years later at seventy-two years of age. Verne recovered and lived until March 1978, when he died at age eighty-two. It was from Verne that my brother Peter and I bought the woollen mill in the late summer of 1970.

THE LAST OF THE MILLERS

When Benjamin Miller died in 1858, he left the hotel in Colborne Mills (Benmiller) to his brother Daniel, who continued to operate it until his death sometime in the late 1860s. Dan's son Jonathan, who was a slim young chap in his twenties when he took it over, soon attained notoriety as the largest man in Huron County. He was a mere 486 pounds, 6 feet 2 inches in height, and had a chest of 84 inches. His wife was apparently no sylph either and they had to have such things as reinforced seats on buggies and carriages specially built for them. In 1877 Jonathan built a large

Jonathan Miller, nephew of Ben Miller, was the largest man in Huron County. He weighed 486 pounds, was 6 feet 2 inches in height and had a chest of 84 inches. A blow-up of this photo hangs in the entrance of the River Mill.

athan and the casket out. One has an image of the twelve pallbearers buckling under the combined weight of Jonathan and the casket.

As Jonathan died childless, it was only through his sister Sally, who married Edwin Gledhill, that Benjamin Miller's lineage continued. The Fisher lineage, on the other hand, is well established throughout the Goderich area, as all of Michael's seven sons remained to farm their 300 acres of land.

Ben Miller's grist mill passed to his son Archibald, but it remained only a short time in his hands, for in the early 1860s he sold it to David Rodgers and left the area for ever. In 1873 it was bought by Michael Pfrimmer, who had come from Germany with his parents at an early age. Not being a miller by trade, he hired David Rodgers, the former owner, to operate the mill for him while he continued to farm. The roller process was introduced at the grist mill in 1890 but the old stones were still used for grinding the grain. In 1910 Michael's son Ernest took over and thoroughly modernized the mill. (This mill is now known as the River Mill.) During World War II the mill was diesel-powered for wartime production but this was only a temporary measure for the mill soon went back to the never-failing power of Sharpe's Creek.

In 1952 Ernest sold out to his sons Russell and Elwyn. The elder Pfrimmer continued to lead an active life until his death in 1963. By this time the grist mill was producing very little and in 1971 Peter and I purchased it from the Pfrimmer brothers.

A BUSTLING VILLAGE

In 1876, eighteen years after Ben Miller's death, the name of the village was changed from Colborne Mills to Benmiller. By then the village was the scene of much industrial activity. There were the grist and woollen mills located on Sharpe's Creek only a few yards apart. There was a nursery with a large greenhouse at the top of the hill beside Joseph Miller's farm. This nursery was purchased in 1863 by John Stewart,

addition to the hotel, which included a grocery store and post office. A Goderich newspaper ran an article saying that "Mr. Miller increased his stable accommodation so that in every particular the Benmiller Hotel is indeed a first-class stopping place." When Jonathan died in 1910 at the age of sixty-one, his casket weighed 455 pounds empty. It had twelve carrying handles and the doorframe of the house had to be widened to get the casket into the house and Jon-

The Pfrimmer grist mill at the turn of the century, and as it appeared when Peter and I bought it. (Top photo: Huron County Museum)

Big Bridge Ben Miller.

The top photo shows Benmiller Village in 1880. In the centre is Jonathan Miller's hotel. To the left is the Pfrimmer house that was renovated in 1973 and later converted into two suites and two separate bedrooms, forming part of the Benmiller Inn complex. In the foreground is the Benmiller Waggon Shop and behind it the wooden flume carrying water from Sharpe's Creek to the grist mill. To the right, part way up the hill, can be seen another Pfrimmer house. At the top of the hill is the nursery. Goose Alley is the road running to the left of the hotel. (Photo: Huron County Museum)

In the sceond photo, Jesse Gledhill is standing on the bridge over the Maitland River. The bridge at this time was fairly new. The old wooden one had been washed away by ice in 1903. The grist mill to the right had just been built. To the left is the old hotel. (Photo courtesy of Dorothy Fisher)

Looking down from Miller's Hill. In the larger photo, taken in the early 1900s, the grist mill is to the left, the Pfrimmer barn is in the foreground and behind it is Jonathan Miller's hotel. To the right of the hotel is the cheese factory and in front of it the Pfrimmer house. (Photo: Huron County Museum)

The second view is a slide taken in 1970 showing both old and new bridges.

The woollen mill at the turn of the century. In the foreground is the fountain that Jesse Gledhill had built, and behind it is the wooden flume running from Sharpe's Creek. The area where sheep are grazing is now completely wooded. In the background to the right is a blacksmith's shop and to the left is the Benmiller General Store. (Photo: Huron County Museum)

This view shows the original two-span wooden bridge across the Maitland River which was washed away by ice floes in 1903. In the centre of the photo is the crowded little street known as Goose Alley. At the far right is Geisbuch's tannery. Next is Gotfried Maedal, also a tanner. Next is the house of Rodney Adams, who made grain cradles, and then Jake Hediger, the painter. At the end of the street is the Pfrimmer house (now Mill House). Facing is the grist mill (now the River Mill). The hotel and cheese factory are on the left. This photo has been blown up to mural size (8 feet by 10 feet) and is on the upper wall of the present-day swimming pool. (Photo: Huron County Museum)

Jonathan Miller's hotel. Jonathan is seated on a chair at the corner of the building. (Photo: Huron County Museum)

The Benmiller blacksmith shop, 1890. (Photo: Huron County Museum)

The Benmiller General Store.
(Photo courtesy of Dorothy Fisher)

(Right) House originally built by a
Gledhill and later lived in by a
Pfrimmer. (Photo courtesy of
Dorothy Fisher)

(Below) The old schoolhouse.
(Photo courtesy of Dorothy Fisher)

Gotfried Maedal's house, now
abandoned and soon to be torn
down. (Photo: Bluewater
Photography)

The present-day manager's house was once occupied by Willa and Verne Gledhill. (Photo: Bluewater Photography)

whose son Joseph spent his life enlarging it into one of the best in the country. In its heyday it had four travelling salesmen representing it throughout the province. Joseph died in 1960 without anyone to carry on the business.

On the other side of Joseph Miller's farm was Andrew Heddle, the carpenter, who built many of the sturdy houses in the neighbourhood, several of which still stand. Beside him lived Frederic Larmey, the tailor, who went from house to house making men's and boys' suits of full cloth. Across from him lived Fred Speight, the weaver. Further along was the little log schoolhouse, later replaced by a frame one built by Andrew Heddle. Beside the schoolhouse lived the schoolmaster, Arthur Molesworth, and across from him was Thomas Kerr, the shoemaker. Directly opposite at the other corner was the Benmiller Presbyterian church built in the late 1860s by Heddle.

Jonathan Miller's hotel was on the corner opposite the Pfrimmer grist mill, beside a crowded little street by the Maitland River known as Goose Alley because of Gotfried Maedal's geese (and referred to by some locals as Goose Turd Alley). Maedal was a tanner by trade and his house still stands abandoned and soon to be torn down. Beside him was Geisbuch's tannery. Here also was De Gray, the cooper, who made fine barrels, and Rodney Adams, famous for his grain cradles. Thomas Good's stone lime kiln was also situated along the river's edge, as well as the house of Jake Hediger, the painter.

Part way up the hill toward the greenhouse, next to the hotel, was John Durst, the blacksmith, who made wagons as well. There was a cheese factory and two general stores and near the woollen mill was Joshua Moore, the shoemaker. There were about fifteen homes interspersed among all these industries. The village even boasted a small orchestra of string players. The first postmaster was Edwin Gledhill but later the post office moved to Mary Miller's grocery store. A stage coach ran daily from Goderich with the mail. Benmiller had become a perfect example of a self-contained pioneer community. With few exceptions, everything necessary for existence was provided by someone within the village.

By 1858 the railway had come to Goderich, bypassing Benmiller. The early settler was always faced with the struggle for better communication with the outside world—to bring in needed goods and equipment and to send out produce. With the railway came improved access to markets. People could afford to buy silk and cotton in place of homespun, bakeshop bread in place of flour from the grist mill, shoes in Goderich instead of those hand-made by the local shoemaker. One by one the industries in Benmiller moved away or closed down. The tannery moved to Saltford, the blacksmith Fisher to Kincardine. No one stayed overnight in Jonathan Miller's hotel so he went to operate the Hotel Bedford in Goderich in 1896. In 1912 telephones came to Colborne Township. The system had eleven circuits with the switchboard in the Benmiller General Store.

The village even boasted a small orchestra, mainly of string players. Standing at the back is George James. In the second row, left to right, are Harry Mew, Walter Straughan, George Stewart, Arthur Fisher and Tom Johns. In front are Dick Heddle and Harry Gledhill.

On the second floor of the woollen mill, 1925-30. Verne Gledhill is at the winder or "mule" at left and Percy Walters at right centre. Verne is holding a small animal, perhaps a pig? (Photo courtesy of Dorothy Fisher)

Finally by 1935 only the grist and woollen mills were operating, and they too were doomed. By 1970 there was no commercial activity in Benmiller except a welding shop and, across from it, the Benmiller General Store, which was just that: it supplied everything for the home—fresh produce, basic drugstore supplies, clothing, hardware, even gas for cars. From a thriving pioneer village, Benmiller had become a quiet little hamlet of but a dozen homes. By 1975 even the store had to close down because a large supermarket built on the outskirts of Goderich on Highway 8 took away what little business it still had.

The one thing that has never changed in the village of Benmiller is its natural and unique beauty.

Ray Moore at the spinning wheel. (Photo courtesy of James Lafer/Margaret Garbarino)

In this lovely set of photos taken in the 1950s, Clyde Gledhill is setting up the winder (left) and Ray Moore is seen at the loom (lower left). Verne Gledhill (lower right) operates the mule. (Photos courtesy of James Lafer/Margaret Garbarino)

The Woollen Mill

Behind the mill were 200 feet of wood and concrete racks used for drying and stretching the blankets in fair weather. (Photo courtesy of Dorothy Fisher)

Peter and Joanne with Verne Gledhill shortly after they purchased the woollen mill. (Photo courtesy of Cleeve Horne)

A MOMENT OF MADNESS

What attracted my brother and me to the village of Benmiller? What prompted us to renovate two 100-year-old mills and two millers' houses into an inn, to plunge headlong and, as our father said, foolhardily, into the extremely competitive hospitality business?

Peter's answer was always, "It was just a moment of madness." For me, it just happened. Peter just happened on the woollen mill when it came up for sale. We both just happened to be at the same spot and both just happened to be looking for something—Peter for some old beams and I for a project.

Peter was a businessman, involved in running the family's plumbing business in London, Ontario. I, though educated in the visual arts, had spent most of my life doing what I loved best, singing. It was small wonder that people asked us why we would choose something in which neither of us had any experience or formal training. My husband had died in 1968, two years before we purchased the woollen mill, and I was desperately looking for a challenge. I had recently bought and renovated two little houses across the street from where I lived in Toronto, so real estate was very much on my mind.

At the same time, Peter wanted to build a cabin near his cottage for a couple he had employed. He wanted to use old hand-hewn beams and barn board and had seen an ad in the London paper offering for sale the timber from an old barn in Carlow, a village just north of Benmiller.

The woollen mill painted by the late Jack McLaren shortly before the mill was sold.

As it was late August Peter and I were both at our cottages at Grand Bend, about three-quarters of an hour's drive south of Benmiller. Before Peter left to take a look at the old barn in Carlow, I asked him if I could have a small piece of a beam to use as a mantel over the fireplace in one of my renovated houses. When he returned some hours later, he dropped in to report that he had bought the barn and the beams were in excellent condition. (The beams and barn board never did become the cabin they had been intended for. They can be seen holding up the dining room of Benmiller Inn.) He casually mentioned that he had passed through the village of Benmiller and had seen a "for sale" sign on a post in front of the old woollen mill.

I was immediately interested, for when we were young Mother had taken us to Benmiller at least once a summer to buy a blanket or just to picnic around the fountain. The greatest treat was to go inside and watch the big looms at work. I still remember Clyde Gledhill and Ray Moore bending over the looms and Verne Gledhill upstairs at the winder. Clyde was tall and slim and his brother Verne was shorter and more solid. You certainly knew all three were related, for they all had the same strong roman-looking nose.

I offered Peter a drink and we sat down to reminisce. Whether it was the alcohol or nostalgia I don't know, but before long we were planning the renovation of the woollen mill. It had become a little English-style inn nestled in the lovely hollow of Benmiller, covered with ivy and surrounded by a rail fence and rose bushes. Peter had been in England during the war and had fallen in love with English wayside inns. At this point we weren't really serious, but I was curious to see what the old place looked like.

The next day Peter was off to Montreal on business and I was off to Benmiller. I asked my father, who was visiting me, if he would like to go for a drive.

There wasn't a soul around when we arrived at the woollen mill. The setting was as lovely as I had remembered, but what a sad sight to see a once-lively and productive building silent and decaying. I peered in the windows through a thick layer of dust and cobwebs and saw the motionless looms inside. All the machinery appeared to be there, undisturbed. I could see the dusty rose-pink wool still on the spools of the looms, the colour that was unique to the Benmiller blankets. The old mill looked so sad, so deserted and the "for sale" sign so large and so commanding, I wrote down the name and the telephone number of the agent. I was curious to know how much they were asking for the mill.

When we arrived home, I went immediately to telephone, to satisfy my curiosity. When I heard what they were asking I was amazed. It seemed a gift, but when I told my father later about my phone call he thought differently. "If you bought it, no matter what the price or what you planned to do with it, you'd have a sink-hole on your hands." But at that moment I didn't hear his wise counsel.

My next move was to call Peter. I told him what I had done and that I felt we should buy the mill immediately before someone else snapped it up. Peter told me not to rush into it. He would be home in a few days and we could discuss it at length then. I was sure by that time it would be too late as there was another potential buyer seriously interested in the building.

"All right, Peter," I said. "If you don't want it, I'll buy it and *then* we can discuss it."

"O.K.—but make sure you strike a good bargain," he said. I assured him that that was no problem as I felt it was already a good bargain.

Before our offer would be accepted, the agent told me, we would have to discuss it with the present owner, Verne Gledhill.

The mill had been shut down for eight years. There had been talk of making all of Benmiller into a pioneer village and the woollen mill would play a key role in this plan. Jack McLaren, an artist who had a few years earlier moved to Benmiller from Toronto and who was president of the local historical society, saw the village's potential, but the society was unable to agree on plans or a price. Verne Gledhill, who was fed up with waiting as he was seventy-four years old and getting no younger, just wanted to get his affairs in order.

I told Verne that my brother and I would very much like to buy the mill and that we had a vague idea of making it into a country inn. I had the feeling, after talking with him, that he really didn't mind what we did with it as long as we didn't turn it into a turnip factory. I paid our down payment and signed on the dotted line.

The next weekend, when Peter came back to Grand Bend, we immediately went to Benmiller to see Verne. He took us over to the mill and I'll never forget my excitement when he pulled the great arm that put the huge network of pulleys and belts into motion. The old wooden planks started to quiver and vibrate under our feet. We were instantly surrounded by a loud thundering of groaning and whirring sounds, the sound of heavy machinery being activated after eight years' silence. I was aware of the faint musty lanolin smell of oiled fleece. Soon the large wheels were purring as they had done for over 100 years.

Verne showed us how the huge looms and the carding machine operated and the shed where the large vats were kept for dyeing the wool. Peter was as excited as I was and he and Verne got along so well that I'm sure Verne wouldn't have minded if we *had* decided to wax turnips. As long as Verne lived, these two men enjoyed a feeling of respect and affection for each other.

As we left Benmiller that day, the agent said, "You know, I think, if you were interested, the grist mill down by the river could be for sale."

Peter and I looked at each other and said in unison, "No way. One is enough."

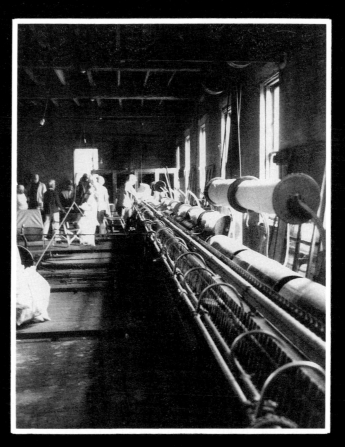

Inside the woollen mill shortly after we bought it. (Clock-wise from top left) The main drive wheel, which is now part of the dining room wall nearest Sharpe's Creek; it serves as a window at the top of the circular stairs. The winder machine. The bobbin machine that fed the smaller loom. A spinning wheel. The carding machine. (Photos courtesy of Cleeve Horne)

We wouldn't have considered buying the grist mill as the bridge across the Maitland River was then further downriver and the road went very close to the side of the mill. The second photo shows the new and the old bridges in 1972.

By January 1971, just four months later, we had bought the grist mill as well. We wouldn't have considered such a purchase when we first arrived on the scene, for the bridge across the Maitland was then further downriver and the road went very close to the side of the mill, making it useless as a residence. When we were told that the bridge was to be moved the next year to a site well upriver east of the mill, we reconsidered.

FIRST MOVES

Peter and I now had two mills on our hands and the question was what to do with them. We had our own lives to lead and neither of us lived near Benmiller.

During that first winter there was relatively little activity on the site. It was a time to get to know the countryside and the people. From the outset Peter fitted easily into the community. Though always busy, he took the trouble to get to know our neighbours—not for political reasons but because he liked the local people and was interested in what they thought and how they felt. Because of this, for the most part we were accepted and trusted. The local people understood that we were not about to destroy the unspoiled beauty that had lured us to the village of Benmiller in the first place.

It was also a time for rumours. One was that Benmiller had been bought by the Mafia (I suppose a natural assumption as my married name was Mazzoleni). Another was that rich people from the city had bought it for one of "those clubs" for their friends. We read in several local papers that the mills were to become a centre for arts and crafts. Then we heard the woollen mill was to be a mansion or night club. We soon learned that when one becomes part of a small community, rumours are a way of life.

We were nearly forced into becoming one of "those clubs," for when we bought the mills Colborne Township was dry. A vote was requested by the Machinists Union in 1971 and the bid was defeated. It

The concrete of both dams needed patching and the flood gate apparatus repairing. Shown here is the upper dam above the woollen mill during and after repairs. (Lower photo: Bluewater Photography)

The flow from Sharpe's Creek was diverted during heavy runs by the installation of a flood gate part way up the hill beside the present dining area. (Photo: Bluewater Photography)

The lower dam after it had been rebuilt. (Photo: Bluewater Photography)

could not be put to the vote again until 1973. Fortunately for us, all was resolved by the time we opened, for if the township had remained dry, the only way we could have had a liquor licence would have been as a private club.

Peter's first move was to put in a mobile home on the north side of the woollen mill to be used as an office. We still had no idea what we were going to do. Indeed, the feeling that we never would do anything with the mills seldom left me those first few months. That was before I had seen my brother in action. His next move was to employ someone to take a complete set of black and white photos of both mills, including detailed shots of all the machinery. From these I had blow-ups made which later were to hang in the dining area of the Woollen Mill and in the bridge connecting the swimming pool with the River Mill.

At the same time Peter arranged for the repair of the mud gate apparatuses on both dams as well as patching the concrete, which was badly cracked. He had noticed that both ponds were badly silted and was worried that their effectiveness as flood control reservoirs had been impaired, so he made arrangements to have them dredged. This turned out to be an extensive and expensive operation. A few years later, the foundation of the dining room and kitchen areas along with the supports for the penstock pipe created a major constriction in the stream bed during heavy run-off. Peter diverted the water so that when it rose behind the dam, even with the mud gate open, it would flow faster up the bank running beside Sharpe's Creek. At the end of this flow, he installed an extra flood control gate. To make sure the penstock control gate opened properly he had to put a screen in front of the gate to stop debris. If there was ever any sign of a prolonged thaw, then the mud gates on both the upper and lower dams had to be opened. About this time Peter divided the upper pond into two parts, creating a trout pond on the west side and a steady stream of water over the dam on the other. In the early years of the Inn we stocked the west pond with fish so that guests could catch their own breakfast. Along the earth walkway which was created down the centre of the pond we planted weeping willows. These in later years have become something of a hazard for the angler casting for fish, though they look very beautiful.

The first significant activity took place the following spring. When we purchased the woollen mill, it was understood that the township would need ten feet of our property on both sides of the road to the north, by the upper dam, because they were planning to build a new bridge. To do this they would have to block the entrance to the mill. For compensation they offered to put in a new entrance to the south. This was a bit of luck for the land they took we didn't need but the new road into the mill from the south we did, for it was obvious that no matter what the woollen mill was to become, the entrance would have to be changed.

At one time Peter had entertained the idea of going into the business of bottling water, for there were over a dozen springs gushing out of the hill to the north. When the township built the new bridge and road however, the digging disturbed the land formation enough to dissipate the flow of the springs.

THE POINT OF NO RETURN

When I went to Benmiller one weekend early that summer, to my surprise the woollen mill was teeming with activity. Young men were running around with great pieces of iron on their shoulders. They were loading all the beautiful iron and wooden pulleys into a truck and hauling them away. Peter had hired four local boys and two nephews to clear the mill of the machinery. One of these local boys, fresh out of high school, was to stay with us throughout the whole building project. Brad Vanstone remained to guide the maintenance staff expertly through our most dif-

ficult years, a task that would have been formidable for someone twice his age.

Once I had found out that the precious cargo was not going to the dump but to the barn near the present-day tennis courts, I relaxed somewhat. (We acquired the barn and "Upper Lands West" at the same time we purchased the grist mill, now known as the River Mill.) The one item I was unable to save was an old pine plank with two large well-worn holes in it that came from the back of the mill. Perhaps it's as well that the boys burned the two-holer, for I had thought it would make a lovely coffee table with two large pots of geraniums stuffed into the holes. As things turned out this would have been inappropriate for the lobby of Benmiller Inn.

By the fall of 1971 it was apparent that we were going to do something with the mills, though we weren't sure whether it would be a club or a hotel. One thing Peter and I agreed upon was that it would have to be a very special place—the most comfortable, interesting, attractive place we could create in order to attract people to a spot that was relatively unknown and over two hours' drive from any large urban centre—an "adult oasis," as Peter called it.

The first drawings were handed to me in February of 1972. These were the builders' plans from Peter's designs, and I was soon to grow very familiar with the many revised drawings done in Peter's own hand, for I learned that whenever one does a complex renovation, one is continually faced with surprises and each surprise has to be resolved with more plans. I had to empty my briefcase weekly to make room for new ones.

The renovation of the Woollen Mill began in April 1972. The first thing to go was the shed at the back of the mill where the turbine and the huge dye vats were housed. The water power system was retained but the old turbine was replaced with a 1910 75-horsepower turbine from Barrie, Ontario, so that the whole system could be put into operation at any time. A concrete

The water power system was retained but the old turbine was replaced with a 1910 75-horsepower turbine so that the whole system could be put into operation at any time.

A concrete foundation was poured close to Sharpe's Creek and on top went a plywood flooring leaving the turbine and dye vats underneath.

The structure was of post and beam construction, using the old beams from the Carlow barn.

The new structure was extended from the main building on the creek side where the shed had once been.

foundation for the dining and kitchen area was poured as close to Sharpe's Creek as possible so that the pleasure of eating beside this fast-flowing stream could be shared by many people. On top of this foundation went a plywood flooring, leaving the turbine and old dye vats underneath. These can still be seen in the basement under the dining room and kitchen. The creek-side dining room wall was built around the flume and one can look down through a port hole window at the top of the circular stairs to see water from Sharpe's Creek running through it.

The new structure was extended from the main building and the entrance was off the bar area. This was later changed when the solarium was added. The structure was of post and beam construction, the exterior being of random-width barn board with vertical cover strips. It had much the same appearance from the outside as the original shed but was much larger. From the inside the dining room had a natural look of

We took the dining room as close to Sharpe's Creek as we could so that the pleasure of eating beside the fast-flowing stream could be shared by as many people as possible.

(Left) Men at work on the roof of the dining room.

Our old Carlow posts and beams (above) melded perfectly with the straw plaster in between, giving the interior a natural look of antiquity. (Photo: Bluewater Photography)

The exterior is of random-width barn board with vertical cover strips. The large round window was the main drive pulley for all the machinery in the mill. (Photo: Bluewater Photography)

antiquity. Our old Carlow barn posts and beams melded perfectly with the straw plaster in between. The large round window on the exterior wall of the dining room at the top of the circular stairs had been the main drive pulley for all the machinery in the mill.

The old planking from the floor of the main building was removed. The pine planks unfortunately were in such poor condition that they were not worth saving. A front-end loader moved inside the mill and dug out the earth to a depth of about four feet. Steel girders, which had been salvaged from the old bridge across the Maitland River the summer before, were laid at twelve-foot intervals four feet above the earth floor.

Peter had always been fascinated with the silo concept and from the beginning had decided the best way to treat the open space of this large building was to build a silo up the centre for storage and to house all the mechanics. The concrete was poured for the base of the silo and for the fireplaces at either side of it. Then, concrete block by concrete block, the silo went up the centre of the building, the circular staircase of steel treads being imbedded step by step as it went up.

Fourteen-foot joists of two-by-twelve lumber were laid at one-foot intervals across the girders, and on top of them sheets of plywood, leaving a crawl space under the floor of four feet. The original posts, which had been removed when the planking was taken out, were carefully put back to support the original ceiling beams. The posts had started to rot at one end so Peter had them trimmed back a foot and added a shaped detail at the top that immeasurably enhanced the overall appearance. The detail was carved from old beams he had recently purchased from a salvage company. In between the twelve-inch beams were exposed three-by-ten-inch joists. The drywall between the joists was slightly arched with plaster to give a softening effect. The two inches of mortar and flagstone that went on top of the plywood

The earth was dug out to a depth of four feet. Steel girders salvaged from the old bridge across the Maitland River were laid at twelve-foot intervals, and a concrete foundation was poured for the silo and the fireplaces at either side of it.

Concrete block by concrete block, the silo went up the centre of the building. As well as supporting the risers of the circular staircase, it provided space inside for storage and mechanicals.

The large fireplace on the lobby side of the silo. The circular staircase of steel treads was embedded step by step as the silo went up.

In this view, just inside the entrance looking towards the bar area, the silo has been completed at the right. The subfloor has been laid and posts have been put back in place.

The original posts had to be trimmed because they had started to rot at the ends. A shaped detail was added at the top which enhanced the overall appearance. (Photo: Bluewater Photography)

While construction of the dining room was going on, fourteen dormers were cut into the roof of the main building, supported by the end walls and five equally spaced A-frames.

In the foreground of the bottom photo are the concrete posts that were used to stretch and dry the blankets.

subfloor were the last things to be done before the mill opened its doors for business. The overall effect was one of aged mellowness.

On the top floor of the main building, fourteen dormers were cut into the original pitched roof one by one, supported by the end walls and by five equally spaced A-frames. The bedrooms on the second and third floors were roughed in, each one having its own shape and character. The ones on the third floor presented a particular challenge because of the A-frame beams and the dormers. For this reason I think they turned out to be the most interesting. In the bedrooms we used the barnboard from Peter's barn. The cupboards, the doors and the door trim were all made of barn-board. The baseboard was vertical strips of the board. The bedheads were barn-board as well, with wrought iron pieces in the design of our future logo placed on top. We soon used up all of the Carlow barn and by the time we finished we had purchased several more as well.

The wrought iron over the bedhead was not local. It had come from a "widow's walk" on top of the old Customs House in downtown London, Ontario. This building had been torn down just before we purchased the mills. Peter had been given all the stone and iron for the price of hauling it away and unknown to me had stored the iron in our barn. He had forgotten about it until we needed something to finish off the beam over the bar in the lobby. When he first showed it to me, the wrought iron was covered with white paint and most unprepossessing. Once it was stripped of its paint, it was extremely handsome and

Because of the A-frames and dormers, the bedrooms on the third floor turned out to be the most interesting. The base board is vertical strips of barn-board. The mirror is an old hay fork. (Photo: Bluewater Photography)

The wrought iron over the bedhead came from the widow's walk atop the old Customs House in downtown London, Ontario. This later became our logo. The pillows on the barn-board bedhead came from material that was printed from an original etching of the Woollen Mill. This material was to have covered the wall up the circular staircase until the fire marshal vetoed it. (Photo: Bluewater Photography)

My first surprise was the totem pole, carved in the early 1960s by an Indian on Vancouver Island.

Facing page
Interior views of the Woollen Mill.

we used it extensively throughout the mill as an accent.

My first real surprise was the totem pole that arrived in the late fall of 1972. It had been carved in the early 1960s by an Indian on Vancouver Island.

"What is that?" I asked Peter. I had never envisaged a totem pole in the middle of Benmiller. It was one of the few times we hadn't seen eye to eye on aesthetics. I was wrong, though, for I have grown to love that pole. It has weathered beautifully and it somehow sets the terrace off.

Summer, fall and winter came and went. The work progressed slowly. In fact, the renovation of the woollen mill seemed to take forever. In retrospect I don't think anyone was to blame. Peter had not yet retired from his business; his infrequent visits that summer and throughout the next winter always caused a flurry of activity after which work would go back to a grinding halt. One can't really blame the workmen either. Peter set very high standards and because of the nature of the project, someone should have been at the site at all times and I was not experienced enough for such a position.

It became my job to make sure the carpeting and wallpapers would be there when needed and to show the plasterers how to do the straw and rough plastering. I had used straw plaster in one of my houses in Toronto with great success and Peter had insisted we use it in the mill. Straw plastering was used in peasant houses in England many years ago. The straw helped to bind the plaster to the walls. It is executed by facing the rough plastered wall with a bale of straw close at hand. You take a handful of this straw and throw it on the wall with as much abandon as possible. Then, with a trowel, you remove the loose bits. It was difficult to find the right man for the job as each had his own way of tackling the challenge. Some resisted outright, some were too careful and only one man had the freedom required for the job. We used straw plaster in the dining room as well as on all the

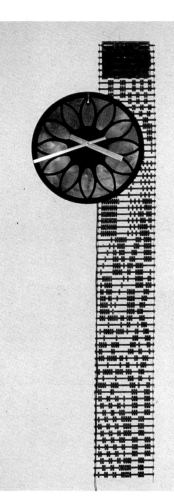

A wall sconce in one of the third-floor suites. The backing for this wheel was taken from an old plough. (Photo: Bluewater Photography)

A wall sconce in the front lobby made from a wheel from a carding machine.

The clock on the wall to the right of the front desk was made from a wheel from a carding machine. The iron belt beside it was the programming tape of an 1875 broad loom.

The coffee table in the photo above was made from a medium-size wooden pulley. The lamp table is from half a wooden pulley. The photo at left shows the coffee table in front of the large fireplace by the front desk. It was the base for the sifter in the River Mill. (Photo above: Les Langford. Left: Bluewater Photography)

Wall sconce made from a gear. (Photo: Bluewater Photography)

The chandelier in the dining room was made from a large wooden pulley. (Photo: Bluewater Photography)

The photo at right shows a small chandelier in the dining room made from a small wooden pulley with bits of wood removed. The centre is lined with plexiglass. (Photo: Bluewater Photography)

The English pine book case in the lobby near the front desk. (Photo: Bluewater Photography)

inside walls throughout the mill. On the exterior walls, insulation was applied directly to the concrete walls and covered with a special aluminium fireproof paint before the final off-white coat was applied.

We had decided from the outset, before we cleared the building of machinery, that we should put as much of it back into the mill as possible. To help with this, we hired a young graduate of the design course at the Ontario College of Art, Arthur Horne. Using all those marvellous old pieces of wood and iron would require taste and imagination and Arthur had these qualities in abundance. We were not disappointed. It was Arthur who designed and executed the wall sconces, the chandeliers, the bar tables and the lamps. The wonderful clock near the front desk where guests register was his as well. It was made from an old wheel of a carding machine that looked like a daisy with twelve petals. The iron belt hanging down beside the face of the clock was the programming tape of an 1875 broad loom—a most ingenious design. The large and small wooden pulleys used for chandeliers, side tables and coffee tables had been parts of the leather-belt-driven power transmission system in both mills. The iron chandeliers in the lobby were the end frames of a wool processing drum. Through Arthur's eyes I began to see the wealth of things available and how to make use of them.

THE ENGLISH FURNITURE

Our first furniture purchase is a painful part of the story, and a testament to our inexperience. On a trip to England Peter saw an ad in *The Times,* "For Sale— Early English antique pine furniture—very reasonable."

When he arrived home, he phoned me. "I think I've made a find and I'd like to talk to you about it." He said there were two warehouses full of antique pine furniture, each piece more beautiful than the last, all restored and refinished and so reasonable that he couldn't believe it. He said that we should go to

London for a day or two and select all the furniture we might need for the mills.

From the first we had thought of using pine furniture, but we wanted the real thing, the lovely, good old pieces. This seemed an opportunity to pick up all the furniture at once and not have to spend months searching out piece after piece.

We took an overnight flight and upon arrival immediately headed for the warehouses. Never having bought more than one piece of furniture at a time, the experience of selecting a hundred antique chairs, twenty chests, thirty tables, book cases, armoires and so on at one time made my head spin. Peter had been right. The furniture was beautiful and reasonable in price. The next day we were home, exhausted, but elated with our purchases. The furniture was to be shipped in two large containers to arrive in two months.

August and September went by. Finally one container arrived after many letters and phone calls across the Atlantic. It was filled with the "special pieces"—the book shelves, cabinets and chests—but contained none of the tables and chairs for the dining room. We were, however, assured that the other container was on its way.

October went by, then November, and still no container. I began to panic. Then came word from England. Our friend across the water had declared himself bankrupt. A potential backer had taken one look at the books and told him that he was insolvent. His assets were seized and put up for auction. Along with "his" assets went "our" pre-paid furniture.

The backer promptly formed a new company with the original owner as an employee. It wasn't until February of the next year, three months later and a month before we finally opened, that the situation was resolved. If we would pay one thousand pounds we could have our furniture. In other words, buy it back. They would then ship it to us immediately, at our expense. Better still, we could buy more furniture at one-third the purchase price, this offer being good

This breakfront in the dining room was one of the larger English pine pieces. (Photo: Bluewater Photography)

One of the special English pieces, this penny ball machine (left) came from an old pub. It is now part of the bar. The second photo shows an old ship's lantern which hangs in the solarium. (Both photos: Bluewater Photography)

for one year. The furniture finally arrived intact, too late to be used for the Woollen Mill. It was stored along with my other treasures in the barn until it could be used in the River Mill. As it happened, it was a good thing the tables and chairs arrived too late to be used in the dining room, for they would have been a great mistake. Though the tables were handsome, they would have made our dining room look more like a country kitchen and the hundred-year-old English chairs soon fell apart in our dry atmosphere and had to be abandoned. The tables on the other hand were perfect for the bedrooms of the River Mill.

In November, when I realized we had no tables and chairs for the dining room, I knew something had to be done. With Kitchener and Stratford, the furniture centres of western Ontario, relatively close, I turned my attention in that direction. A furniture factory in Kitchener had seventy-five unfinished chairs that had been ordered for a steak-house in Stratford. The steak-house didn't need them. They were exactly the shape I wanted and were sturdy and comfortable. We had our own finish and material put on them and they were ready in a month's time. The tables were easy. With good tablecloths, it matters little what you have underneath. They were standard fare.

MORE CRISES

Soon another crisis was on its way. I had had 500 yards of material silk-screened with the original print of the woollen mill on it. It was to be used on the wall around the circular staircase leading to the second floor to add interest. The design of the mill on the material was carefully placed at eye level as you ascended. We were prepared to fireproof it if necessary.

Not only did the fire marshal veto my material, but he vetoed the whole stairway as well. I had 500 yards of material without a home and the opening was delayed by two months while we did the necessary alterations to the stairway. A heavy reinforced glass and steel structure had to be built at the top of the stairs

leading to the second floor and at the bottom of the stairs leading to the third floor to close them in. To accommodate this, the upper halls had to be changed. Doors had to be cut through the cast lime wall on the north side of the building and a large circular staircase installed as an escape. Several years later there was a change in the fire code and we were forced to add another circular staircase to the south side of the building. Aesthetically it turned out for the best, as these staircases greatly enhance the appearance of the building. The 500 yards of vetoed material became lamp shades, menus, album covers, waitresses' aprons and decorator's pillows, and finally the remainder was used on the wall of the gift shop.

As the mill was getting closer to completion, I needed carpenters to help with the final details. This is when our first "works of Art" made their appearance. Art Fowler, one of the carpenters on the construction site, was the only one who understood what I wanted and was able to carry out my directions—with improvements. I never heard him say, "It can't be done." Throughout the whole project, whenever I needed a lamp, a special shelf or a table, it was Art who put them together to my designs. He remained with us "temporarily" after the Woollen Mill, the River Mill and the swimming pool were completed. He was doing "works of Art" for the Gledhill project and remained on the staff of Benmiller Inn as part of the maintenance department until 1987.

Whenever I could get away I would trip around the country searching for special things for the Mill. I bought the beautiful arched corner cabinet in the private dining room, in Nova Scotia. It is a very early classic Acadian piece. Its twin is in Uniacke House, a Nova Scotia provincial museum that has an outstanding collection of original furnishings.

THE LAST BLANKETS

Shortly after we purchased the mill, Verne Gledhill had said that he had in his basement the last fourteen

This divider is to the left as you enter the Woollen Mill. It was part of a bobbin machine which fed the looms. Note the clock in the background. (Photo: Bluewater Photography)

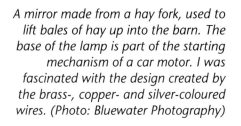

A mirror made from a hay fork, used to lift bales of hay up into the barn. The base of the lamp is part of the starting mechanism of a car motor. I was fascinated with the design created by the brass-, copper- and silver-coloured wires. (Photo: Bluewater Photography)

A standing lamp made from an auger out of the old grist mill. The pole rotated to move the grain along a shute. The base was an iron wheel on the carding machine. These lamps are in the bedrooms of the Woollen Mill. (Photo: Bluewater Photography)

Doors to the private dining room were from the Grand Theatre in London, Ontario. They are almost two inches thick. (Photo: Bluewater Photography)

This corner cabinet in the private dining room is an early Acadian piece, the twin of which is in Uniacke House in Nova Scotia. (Photo: Bluewater Photography)

blankets that had been taken off the looms when the mill shut down in 1964. They had never been finished and were in one long piece. He had stored them in the basement of his home, for at the time he knew of no one who could wash, cut and finish them. He said if I could find someone, they were ours.

It wasn't until the August before we opened that I started to look. I asked a friend who was involved with the Canadian Crafts to see if he could get some information. I had been warned by Verne that whoever did the job would have to have large enough facilities and would have to know how to treat the loose basket-weave characteristic of the Benmiller blankets. After some searching my friend reported that there was a blanket mill in Lachute, Quebec, that could possibly finish them.

I wrote to Lachute, sending them a sample of the blankets, saying that unless they were absolutely sure they would have no problem cutting and finishing them, I would prefer that they not tackle the job as the blankets had a heritage value to us. They wrote back assuring me there was no problem.

I loaded the blanket cloth into my station wagon and headed for Lachute. When I arrived, the manager fortunately was still there, for they had neglected to say in their letter that in August the plant shuts down for two weeks. He said not to worry, that he had a couple of men to help him and that the blankets would be ready the next morning. First thing next morning, I called. He said they were still drying and that for sure they would be ready the next day.

For the next three days I searched the countryside for antiques, each morning checking with the mill first to find out the state of our blankets. Each time he assured me that the blankets would be ready that evening. Finally, on the third day I told them that whether or not the blankets were ready, I would have to leave for home and they could send them to me. He said that I could pick them up any time, for unfortunately they had ruined them.

The weather vane on top of the dining room came from Lachute, Quebec. (Photo: Les Langford)

The small flat field of weeds and straggly trees around the mill before the transformation. (Below) Planting the instant forest.

I couldn't believe he was really serious but when I arrived to pick them up, he wheeled out on a dolly a big mass of misshapen, congealed wool. The blankets were still uncut, and they looked as if they had been boiled in a strong detergent and then put in a hot dryer. I wanted to cry, but what was done was done.

He could see how upset I was. He asked if there wasn't something they could do to make up for the disaster.

"Yes," I said, "you can supply us with enough blankets for our woollen mill at half price." This they did and I took my mass of misshapen wool and went home.

Luckily, Lachute at that time was an antique collectors' dream, for it turned a disastrous trip into a partial success.

LANDSCAPING

While the inside of the mill was slowly taking shape we realized something would have to be done to the field of weeds encircling the building. It now seemed we would be opening that winter; consequently the garden would have to be put in the summer before we opened.

Hans Schmitz had done a beautiful job of laying out my garden in Toronto, as well as the back gardens of the two houses across the street that I had renovated. One of these gardens had won the Landscape Ontario Award of Excellence as the best small garden of the year. Hans did wonderful stone work and had a good eye for space, though his methods of working were slightly unorthodox.

"What had you in mind?" he asked, when I first took him to the mill to see if he would undertake a project so far away from Toronto.

"Well, I had an idea of hollyhocks, daisies, cornflowers. You know, country flowers."

"Those are weeds, not flowers," he said.

"Why do you ask, then?" I snapped. "Just put

something down on paper for my brother to see," for I knew that no matter how primitive the drawing, the results would be more than satisfactory.

His next question was, "How's the fishing at Benmiller?"

"Great," I said, and showed him some fishing pictures to prove it.

"I'll do it. Fishing season is early June. I'll be there."

When Schmitz submitted his plans, complete with costing, Peter was a bit taken aback, for though Hans's design was very simple, his price seemed high. In the end, however, we got a bargain.

Schmitz arrived one day in early June with three other men. He had a school bus converted to a home on wheels, a truck full of gardening tools, another truck loaded with stone and bricks, and yet another with an instant forest. He took over. Benmiller had never seen the like. His *ein, zwei, drei schnell* method of working was in direct contrast to the card-playing that went on inside the mill.

It was the height of the black fly season, but the men seemed impervious to them. They were on the site for the better part of two weeks, in which time they transformed the exterior of the mill completely. From a small flat field of weeds and a few straggly trees, the land became a beautifully terraced, undulating surface. It was wonderful to watch those forty-foot trees take their place among the 100-year-old pines.

One particularly deadly black-flied evening, rain having been forecast for the next day, Schmitz decided he would work through the night. He had half completed the laying of the bricks on the terrace, and he knew that rain would be disastrous at that stage. We flood-lit the place and the men worked on through the night. The next day was one of those flawless days without a cloud in the sky so they worked all through that day as well. By evening the job had been completed and the men collapsed with exhaustion. They had worked thirty-six hours without a break—hard, back-breaking work.

The next day they left in the pouring rain, exhausted, fly-bitten and suffering from heavy colds. Schmitz and his men came back once more in the fall for a few days to do the brick-work around the fountain and in front of the entrance to the mill—and to fish.

FINISHING TOUCHES... OR RECYCLED CONTEMPORARY

By late 1973 things were coming together nicely. The finishing touches were being applied to the bedrooms and bathrooms on the upper two floors. The kitchen was almost completed, the flagstone was being laid in the lobby and bar area and the banquettes in the dining room had been made and were ready for installation. The finishing touches were the most enjoyable part of the exercise. It was like doing a huge jigsaw puzzle, taking beautiful pieces of iron and wood and making them fit into the right place. Spindles and bobbins from the winding machine were used to finish off the top of the banquettes in the dining room and for the dividers in the lobby and bar areas.

When I needed bedside tables, I went to the store of treasures in the barn to pick through the pulleys and wheels. Most of them came in two sections and were held together by large bolts. When halved they made perfect little end tables. As they needed supporting from beneath, the first place I went was Ken Morris's junk yard up on the hill to sift through his scrap iron. There I found an old plough with S-shaped prongs that were perfect for the job. When I needed mirrors, he had hay forks. He had iron plough seats for the bar. He had sheep shears, old spades, shovels, farm implements, thousands of old iron shapes that could be recycled. If you were to attach a label to the kind of design that resulted, I suppose it would be called Recycled Contemporary.

Peter had been sure earlier that year that we

*The final result of the landscapers'
efforts. (Photo: Integrated Graphics)*

*The landscapers came back once more to do the
brick-work around the fountain, which Jesse
Gledhill had built in the early part of the century.*

would be able to have our grand opening at Christmas time, but because of the delay due to fire regulations we knew we would not be able to open before March of the next year. In order to have all the wrinkles and problems ironed out at the expense of friends rather than guests, I decided to go ahead with our own private opening on New Year's Eve by asking a group of friends who had been a source of inspiration through the early years of the project.

To one of them the mill meant something very personal. Violet Kilpatrick Voaden had been born in the area and her first post as a school teacher had been at the little school house in Benmiller back in the early twenties. She had lived with the Gledhills in their home, which is now the centre part of the present-day Gledhill House.

Also some of these friends had actively participated in creating special pieces for the mill. Peter Haworth designed the stained glass panels over the door into the dining room and over the entrance to the River Mill. As well as being a prestigious painter, Peter has been responsible for many of the finest stained glass windows in churches and synagogues throughout Canada. In our panels he incorporated the shapes of spools and spindles from the mill with our logo in the centre. He later told me that the brightly coloured pieces of glass he used in our windows were bits he had saved from the First World War. He had been a pilot and had been shot down over France. He had picked up as many pieces of glass as he could carry from shattered windows of bombed churches.

Sydney Watson designed the wall-hanging to the left as you go in the front door of the Woollen Mill and his wife, Helen, executed it. Syd, who was principal of the Ontario College of Art for many years, and a very fine painter, was also responsible for designing our logo. He did an exact tracing of our Customs House wrought iron, diminished it and that was it.

Betty McKnight, my mother's sister, otherwise known as Gaby (Great Aunt Betty), made the flowered lamp shades and dried flower pictures in the Gledhill House. As well, she was by my side throughout the whole Benmiller project, patiently listening to my lamentations and frustrations, encouraging me all the way.

Jean Horne, a fine sculptor, "threw together" several bits of old iron that she referred to as jokes, but jokes they were not, for they are special works indeed. The bird on the mantle of the large fireplace near the front desk, made of sheep-shears and a small cog wheel from the mill machinery, is one such piece. On the wall beside it hangs another piece, made from the wrought-iron logo upside down, an iron spade, a couple of spikes or large nails, and a small pitchfork. All this became a beautiful eagle in her expert hands. The first pitchfork, a four-pronged one, was stolen about a year after we opened. Art was able to replace it with a three-pronged one which gave it a more sinister look. This time he soldered it securely in place.

There were twelve guests in all who were willing to accept whatever would be dealt to them that New Year's. There were many things unfinished and workmen everywhere. They were laying the flagstone in the lobby and there were planks crisscrossed over most of the floor to protect it from direct contact. Though the upstairs rooms had been more or less finished, they had to be cleaned and the bathrooms were filthy. Debris was everywhere.

Aunt Betty and I arrived the day before New Year's Eve to clean the upstairs as we could find no one else free to do it. I had threatened, months before, that whether the mill was ready or not I was going to have my party. Peter's reaction was, "As long as you don't slow up the work, go ahead, but you'll have to organize it yourself." The chef, who had been hired four months earlier in anticipation of the mill opening for Christmas, was thrilled to have a trial run. He had been complaining for months that he might lose his touch if he was out of action any longer. The

Relaxing in front of the fireplace in the lobby and (below) the original entrance to the dining room with Peter Haworth's stained glass panel above. (Both photos: Integrated Graphics)

(Left) Wall hanging by Sydney Watson which can be seen to the left just inside the front entrance. (Photo: Tom Van Turnhout)

(Lower left) A suite in the upper floor of the Woollen Mill, and (lower right) the room on the top floor of the mill where the manager lived before we opened, showing the dormers and an A-frame. (Photos: Integrated Graphics)

The contributions of friends. (Above) The stained glass windows over the dining room entrance and the doors into the River Mill were done by Peter Haworth.

The wall hanging (left) in the lobby of the Woollen Mill was designed by Sydney Watson and executed by Helen Watson.

The bird on the mantel-piece (right) of the large fireplace in the Woollen Mill, as well as the eagle, made from our upside-down logo, a few nails and a small pitchfork, were done by Jean Horne.

(Lower right) Little lamps made from spools out of the Woollen Mill were at one time on the tables in the dining room. The lamps and their dried-flower lampshades were done by Betty McKnight. (All photos: Bluewater Photography)

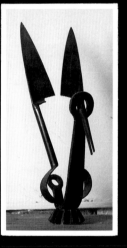

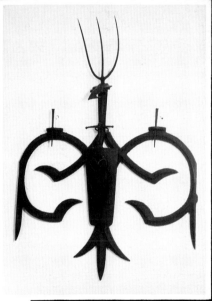

The centrepiece of the chef's lavish buffet for the March 1 opening was a replica of the mill made from sugar cubes and graham crackers.

manager, too, was glad to get going. He and his family had just moved into the newly renovated mill house after having lived for the last four months in one of the rooms on the top floor of the mill.

The kitchen had been in working order for some time. All the dishes, cutlery, pots and pans and linens were in place and ready to go. The private dining room was ready, though the main dining room was far from completed. The furniture was all stacked up and the rug had yet to be laid.

By the time our guests arrived at the front door on New Year's Eve, the workmen were just leaving by the terrace door. Except for the planks in the front lobby and bar area, the place looked open for business. That evening we danced on the uncarpeted wood floor in the dining room and hailed in the New Year to the sound of Guy Lombardo's orchestra on my transistor radio. The chef had prepared samples of all his best fare. We had at least ten soups to try; countless hors d'oeuvres; entrées by the score, every kind of meat and vegetable, to say nothing of his sinful desserts. We were expected to sample a little of everything and comment at length on each delicacy.

New Year's Day, if I remember correctly, we spent most of the time finishing the food left over from the night before. On January 2 at eight o'clock in the morning, the workmen arrived. By the time we made our appearance downstairs the place looked exactly as it had when Aunt Betty and I had entered the mill two days before. There were workmen everywhere laying flagstone, hammering—even the stairs were being dismantled—and we had to gingerly pick our way to the bottom. Breakfast was served at the manager's house before we left for home, as no one could get near the dining room or kitchen. It was only Aunt Betty who suffered from the whole experience, for she always related her deterioration in health to the flu which had downed her the day she left Benmiller.

FINALLY WE OPEN

January and February dragged on. I now spent most of my time at the mill, sleeping in room nine on the top floor. It was a lonely spot at night. My constant companion was my dog, Bijou. Most of the time I was glad to have her at my side, but at night she would constantly utter a low menacing growl, as though someone was creeping around the place. I would strain my ears to hear what she had heard, but could hear nothing, not even a creaking floor board. I would cook my meals in that big kitchen and take a tray into the private dining room. I would sit at the table overlooking Sharpe's Creek, light a candle, and watch the swirling snow mix with the bubbling, fast-flowing stream, and wonder why anyone would want to be in Florida when they could watch nature performing in all its glory at Benmiller.

We planned a grand opening party for March 1, 1974. We invited all the local people plus anyone who had had anything to do with the renovation of the mill. The chef outdid himself, working night and day to put on a buffet the like of which few of our guests had ever seen. He worked around the clock to complete a replica of the mill using sugar cubes and graham crackers.

I shall never forget my father's remark as he walked in the front door the day of the party. It made the long and arduous task of renovating the mill suddenly seem worthwhile. The memory of the frustrations and misgivings disappeared.

"It's absolutely beautiful," he said. Then he remembered I was within hearing distance, so he quickly added, "But it's still a bloody sink-hole." I think, though, that Father was a little proud of what we had done, for later that day, having taken a good look around, he informed me that he would be bringing his friends to Benmiller that weekend to stay.

Father and his eight friends were the first paying guests. All went well the first evening. The chef again performed beautifully, and so did the housekeeping

Peter and Joanne at the front door with an armload of last-minute things.

The front doors of the mill were ready to welcome our first guests March 1, 1974. These doors were designed by Peter to resemble as closely as possible the original ones. The old lamp above was part of our English purchase.

staff. There was an apple beside each bed and the beds neatly turned down.

The first problem arose Sunday morning when Col. X's bath water ended up in Col. Y's tub next door. It turned out that some workmen had carelessly dropped a substantial amount of caulking down the drain and it had lodged at the point where the two drains connected. You can imagine the ribbing my father took from his friends as plumbing had been his life's work, and all our plumbing equipment came from his factory.

We nearly lost our chef over lunch. He particularly wanted to please my father and his guests so he came out of the kitchen to take the order himself, complete with his white hat.

"I would like to prepare something very special for you, Mr. Ivey."

Father, without a moment's hesitation, said, "Do you know what I would like more than anything? I never get it at home. I would love to have some pork and beans. Do you suppose you have a can tucked somewhere around in a back shelf?"

I groaned, and said something like, "He'd better not have," and after lunch went into the kitchen to make my peace.

March, as it turned out, was a good month to open, for it was slow season. It gave us time to iron out the little kinks that are always present with a new project. We still had no liquor licence, and this would have been a far greater problem in peak season. (After constant harassment on our part we finally were granted one on June 27.)

Though we made no attempt at publicity, we were soon inundated with curiosity seekers who just wanted to be "shown through." As the staff were too busy it was my job to conduct tours and direct traffic. There was an endless line of cars driving slowly through the gates. They would circle the fountain several times and then drive out again under the bridge, or just head out the way they came in. We had no directional signs yet so on Sundays there was usually a traffic jam with cars going out the entrance and coming in the exit. Parking became a problem for our guests. Finally I realized I would have to do the signs myself as the maintenance staff had no time and things were getting out of hand. One morning after a long night of sign painting, I went out to see if my signs had been put up and in the right place. To my horror, and the amusement of the maintenance staff, two of them had been misspelled and another had an upside-down "N."

My next attempt at sign-painting was a greater challenge. We needed two large ones for Highway 8, one for west of Benmiller and one for east. They had to be about a quarter of a mile from any other advertising sign on either side of the highway, and they could not exceed a certain size and had to be a certain distance from the highway. The bigger the sign, the further back it had to be. The first problem was to find a spot available within ten miles of Benmiller; the second was to find a farmer who would allow the signs to be put on his property.

The spots were finally found, we had our permits, and I went to work on two eight-foot square pieces of plywood. Art put up a scaffolding in the workshop consisting of two step-ladders with a plank running between them. The signs seemed huge in that confined space. When finally they were finished and put up on Highway 8, I remember my shock when I first saw them, or rather hardly saw them, for they looked like postage stamps.

MEMORIES

So many memories come crowding back of those early days of the Mill, as it was then called. One event that comes to mind was our first wedding. We had been open a little over a month. The ceremony took place in the solarium. It was a beautiful early spring day, warm enough to be outside. Our new garden was bursting into bloom with all the unusual shrubs

Winter at the Woollen Mill with Sharpe's Creek flowing close by the dining room. The forty-foot-long flume pipe is shown entering the dining area. (Photo: Tom Van Turnhout)

Running the tape recorder at our first wedding with a broken arm—from falling off a ladder while stealing for-sythia to keep costs down.

and plants that Schmitz had planted the summer before. I was proud of how beautiful everything looked. For the music the bride had selected the recording of Glenn Gould playing the D Major keyboard concerto of Bach. It was my job to run the record player, which was set up in the bar with the window open between the bar and the solarium. I remember the trouble I had starting and stopping the machine at exactly the right moments, for I had broken my arm the day before, falling off a ladder. I had been stealing my neighbour's forsythia back in Toronto in a frugal attempt to keep the decoration costs of the Mill at a minimum for the bride and groom.

In those early days the manager was forever thinking of new ways in which we could become known, particularly in the Detroit area, as we were only two hours by car away from that city. We had an invitation from the Automobile Club in Grosse Point to give a "little talk." The manager and I drove down with as many slides as I could find of the woollen mill both before and after the renovation. What I didn't know was that we weren't the only ones invited. When we arrived we were told that there would be another couple doing a presentation. They were from Grosse Point and had known the area of Benmiller well, before Peter and I had arrived on the scene. By the time I got to my feet the audience had had enough. A man in the front row, right under my nose, kept nodding his head and falling asleep. This was

disconcerting enough, but when he started to snore intermittently, rather loudly, setting the audience snickering, I decided the time had come to call a halt. That was the first and last time I became involved actively in the promotion of Benmiller Inn.

In those early days we were blessed with very good press, although in at least one instance it wasn't the kind of press we had in mind. A friend asked me one day if I had seen a recent article in a popular magazine on women in the work force and their problems. It described how women were continually being propositioned by their bosses with such things as a "weekend at Benmiller."

Much of our press came from Detroit and the surrounding area and I often had letters from people in Michigan as well as Ontario telling me they had old Benmiller blankets, some dating back to early in this century. Invariably I was asked if I would be interested in buying them (often at an astronomical price). One lady from Michigan wrote that she had a blanket that had been part of her trousseau in the First World War. Her fiancé had been killed and the blanket had been stored in her hope chest ever since. She sent it to me with a little note saying she hoped we could find a use for it as she, sadly, had been unable to. It was a lovely pure white one that had been specially ordered for her by her grandmother.

I spent much of my time at the mill that first year and often checked the guest book, which always sat open on the bar counter. If there were unfavourable remarks, I wanted to make sure they did not go unnoticed. One day I came upon a comment by a friend I hadn't seen for years. It started, "Congratulations, Joanne. You've done a super job. We enjoyed every moment of our stay." Underneath someone else had written, "Who the hell is Joanne?" and the next writer had added, "Who the hell cares?" Not very informative but to the point!

One of the valuable things I learned from the guest book was that many guests were curious to know more about the Mill. In particular they wanted to know what each of the recycled bits of machinery had been. This in part is what prompted me to write this book, albeit many years later.

SKI TRAILS

That winter I concentrated most of my efforts on the ski trails, for I realized that if we were to remain open through the winter we had to have more than just a beautiful building and dining room to attract people. All our neighbours were cooperative in allowing us to go through their land, pruning existing trails and blazing new ones so that even that first winter we had a little skiing to offer. Though at that point they were poorly marked, the trails made up for it in beauty, winding along the valley of the Maitland River. I suppose we had not much more than a few miles of trails, but it was a beginning.

These trails were all to the east of the Inn, but I

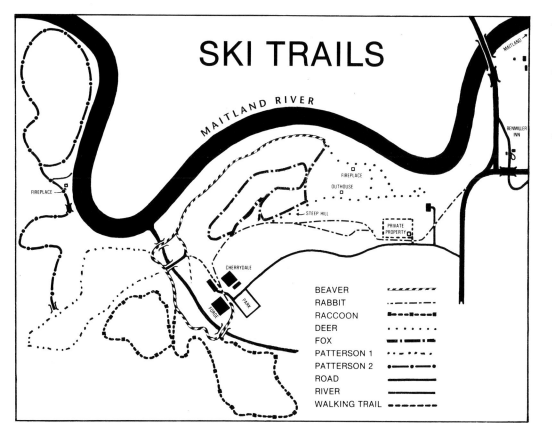

An old oil tank (above) serves as a bridge across the stream behind Cherrydale. The twin of this one is used for water storage for the solar heating system in the Gledhill House.

Benmiller now has many miles of trails through some of the most beautiful land in southern Ontario.

had great hopes of joining up with the trails in the Falls Conservation Area immediately to the west. I knew there were some existing trails in this area, but they were sketchily marked and seemed to go nowhere. I had heard of the "black hole" on the other side of the Falls Area and I knew that if we could get through it, we could ski to Saltford, the little town on the north side of the Maitland, near Goderich. Brad Vanstone, the head of the maintenance department, had lived all his life in Benmiller and knew the bush well. I asked him if he would show me the "black hole" with the idea of blazing a trail through it. "Sure," he said. "How about tomorrow?"

That night when I was dining alone at the Inn, a man approached me. "Aren't you Joanne Ivey? We were at the Ontario College of Art at the same time. I'm here on behalf of *Toronto Calendar* magazine. I'm doing an article on cross country skiing and I understand you are promoting the sport at Benmiller this year."

I told him I was checking out new territory for trails the next morning and asked him if he would like to join me. We set out on a cold, grey early December morning. The ground had a light covering of snow. Once we were past the Conservation Area we were into thick bush. There were occasional indications of foot paths but none of these seemed to lead anywhere. Our guide would head along one of these paths until it came to a fork. He would pause, scratch his head and then with a nod and a grunt of "Uhuh," head in the opposite direction.

After an hour or so of wandering aimlessly through boggy ground and thick underbrush we came upon an old rusty beer can—the same beer can I knew I had seen at least three times before.

"Are you sure your guide knows where he's going?" Obviously my friend had taken note of the beer can as well. I pointed this out to Brad.

"I told you before we started that everyone gets lost down here," he said.

Skier by the Maitland River.

After about four hours of wandering about the bush we finally emerged into the open, many fields from where we had started. I was grateful to my friend from *Toronto Calendar* for taking my word about our trails to the east and their beauty, for he might well have written about getting lost in the bush following non-existent trails at Benmiller instead. I have never been back to the "black hole" since that day and have left the development of the trails to the west to others. Benmiller now has many miles of trails through some of the most beautiful land in southern Ontario.

Fishing on the Maitland River in the Falls area, adjacent to Benmiller. (Photo: Ted Gorsline, Globe and Mail)

The River Mill

Cedar shakes gnawed by rats. (Inset) The grist mill before we purchased it.

Interior of the grist mill when purchased. (Above) The entrance way with the office in the back. The machinery (right) was covered with cobwebs and dust.

WHILE I WAS BUSY painting signs, conducting tours, blazing ski trails—and singing, Peter was hard at work on the plans for the River Mill. This time he hired a contractor from London, Fred Fones, to oversee the job. Work started in November 1974, eight months after the Woollen Mill opened, and we remained on schedule throughout the job.

I remember arriving one morning in the fall to find that the outer parts of the building were being pulled down. Fortunately the inside walls were still standing, for there was a wall that had caught my eye when I first saw the mill. It had once been one of the original outside walls and was covered with old cedar shakes. On a large area of this wall the cedar had been eaten away, creating an interesting three-dimensional design. Legend has it that it had been gnawed by rats trying to get at the grain.

I insisted that the foreman cut out the eight-foot area where the design was the most interesting and store it in the barn with the English furniture (I used to have nightmares that the barn would one day go up in smoke along with our many treasures). Later this bit of wall was trimmed and framed and put back in almost the same place it had been taken from.

When we bought the mill it appeared to be in very poor shape. The exterior was covered with rusted steel siding which had been patched many times. It had a derelict appearance and we wondered

Some of the machinery in the mill when we purchased it.

The exterior was covered with rusted steel siding. The building had a derelict appearance and we wondered if it was worth saving.

The spiral staircase fire escape is one of the striking features of the River Mill.

if the building was worth saving. The inside timber and all the beams, however, were in good condition and we were able to save most of it.

Again we kept the original building in mind during the renovation. What we tore down we built back. As the mill had four floors, we knew we would have to have an elevator. We retained the centre core of the building and attached the elevator to the mill on the road side where a shed had been. What had once been only one storey high, however, we built to the height of the main roof, and in the case of the elevator, it was necessary to take it slightly higher. On the river side we attached an extension much the same as the original, always making sure that each bedroom had large balconies overlooking the river. The construction of the lower two floors was concrete block, the upper two wood with the balconies cut back into the roof.

The base of the mill was made of river stone which we retained and exposed wherever possible. On that lower level were the conference rooms and two bedrooms. Those bedrooms were my favourite for they had a feeling of complete isolation. On one side was Sharpe's Creek cascading over the lower dam and in front was the Maitland River. You could drop a line and catch a fish out of the window on the creek side if you happened to be lucky. Incidentally, Sharpe's Creek is one of the best trout streams in the district and one of the attractions of Benmiller in the spring is to watch the fish jumping many feet into the air in an attempt to clear the dam.

Not long ago, I was visiting the Inn and happened to strike up a conversation with a couple who made a point of staying at the River Mill each year at spawning time. They always stayed on the lower level in the corner room where the mill race runs beneath and the balcony overlooks the spot where Sharpe's Creek joins the river. In the early spring the river often floods and the meeting of creek and river is usually dramatic. They said that the previous year they had

Every room in the mill was designed with either a balcony or a patio. This balcony is off a room on the main floor overlooking Sharpe's Creek and the lower dam.

been fascinated for hours watching the salmon spawn, the males darting back and forth over the eggs. Here was nature at its best, and right beneath their windows.

As the River Mill was a totally different kind of building from the Woollen Mill, we felt that it should have an entirely different feeling about it throughout. We agreed that wherever possible we should expose those marvellous old hand-hewn beams; that oiled cedar siding was the only thing for the exterior; and that the inside should be decorated with the straw and rough plaster we had used in the Woollen Mill. The bridge over the dam was Peter's wonderful idea. Already we were considering an indoor pool to be located next to the mill beside the river and he had rightly visualized the bridge as a way of connecting both buildings with a shared entrance. But what to use for interesting touches for the interior of these buildings? There were bits of the machinery here and there that might prove useful, but for the most part there was little that could be utilized. Then I remembered an exhibition of old pine plumbing patterns at the Art Gallery of Ontario in Toronto a few years back. They had been cleaned and polished and I had been struck by their beauty. I was horrified when Peter told me that just after the war they had burned a whole warehouse of them at the family plant in London when they needed the space.

One day when we were discussing the interior of the mill I said, "What a pity you burned all those old plumbing patterns. They would have been perfect for the River Mill."

"I know where you can get all you want," he casually replied. "The business in London just purchased Darling Bros. foundry in Montreal and they're about to burn a whole warehouse full of patterns for the same reason we did."

The next day I set out for Montreal to visit Darling Bros. I couldn't believe my eyes. Three floors of a huge warehouse contained nothing but old plumbing

Builders at work high over the dam.
(Photos: Karl Roes)

The contruction of the lower two floors on the river side was concrete block.

The upper two floors were of wood construction with the balconies cut back into the roof.

The bridge over the dam was Peter's wonderful idea. It connects the River Mill with the swimming pool. In the first photo, the steel frame can be seen. In the next, the sheathing is on and the wheel window is in place. The elevator, to the right, is the tallest part of the building. The lower views show the interior of the bridge, with its tiled floor, and an exterior shot of the final result.

The fire escape on the west wall from start to finish. This staircase is identical to the ones used in the Woollen Mill. Behind the flagstone wall in the foreground is a patio off one of the main floor bedrooms.

patterns stacked on shelves reaching to the ceiling, some of them dating back seventy to eighty years. They were covered with a thick layer of oily black dirt. The longer I looked, the more excited I became. I selected as many as would fit into my station wagon, and asked the manager not to burn any of them; I would be back in few weeks with a truck. I should have kept the excitement out of my voice, for when I returned a few weeks later, many of the best ones had gone. The word was out.

This time I brought Arthur Horne, who had designed so many of the things in the Woollen Mill. He had an expert eye for design as well as a large van. There were still plenty of the patterns left and we worked feverishly all day, selecting and loading into his van and my station wagon what we could take, and leaving in a pile near the exit what we couldn't. A month later I went back with a large truck and with the exception of the pile we had put aside the place was pretty well cleared out.

Those patterns became the base for the whole interior design of the River Mill. They were so varied and versatile that you could do anything with them. They were modern in concept yet old because of the age of the wood. They seemed to fit in completely with the feeling of the mill. That summer, Art and a young student went to work transforming them into lamps, wall sconces, chests of drawers, room dividers, everything. No matter what we did with them, they seemed to work.

TAKING SHAPE

By the spring of 1975, seven months after the renovations began, the River Mill was taking shape and the time had arrived for the interior details to be attended to. Most important were the windows—what curtaining to use. This had not been a problem in the restoration of the Woollen Mill, for we knew from the start that those windows must have shutters, because of their uniformity and shape. The River Mill was a differ-

At the same time, work was going on inside. In the upper photo the workmen are dividing the space into bedrooms. The lower photo shows the ceiling of the conference room under construction. The river stone walls were exposed in the lower part of the mill.

The view from the bridge is beautiful in all seasons. The spot where Sharpe's Creek meets the Maitland River can be dramatic with the early spring runoff, and the lower corner bedroom has an exciting view.

Fishing at the side of the mill. (Below) Peter and a local fisherman who caught this fine salmon in the Maitland River not far from the mill.

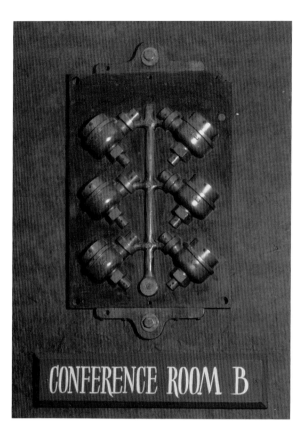

(Left) A wooden plumbing pattern with metal trim on the stairway.

(Right) A solid bronze plumbing pattern on a conference room door in the lower part of the mill. The door was painted by mistake—we had wanted the natural wood to show wherever possible. Rather than having it stripped, we covered it with textured brown leatherette. One of those happy mistakes. (Photo: Bluewater Photography)

CONFERENCE ROOM B

A composition of wooden plumbing patterns in the conference room. (Photo: Bluewater Photography)

The base of this lamp is a wooden pattern.

The window is a round wooden plumbing pattern and the shutters are decorated with a wooden design that was on a piece of machinery taken from the mill. (Photo: Bluewater Photography)

A wooden pattern with metal trim.

This wall sconce on the stairs is two patterns put together.

(Above) This mirror is a combination of two patterns.

(Left) Mirror and wall sconce in a bedroom. (Below) An end table in one of the bedrooms was several patterns put together.

A wooden pattern of a propeller. This wall sconce is on the bridge. (All photos: Bluewater Photography)

(Right) Part of a suite on the second floor showing a post and beam. In the background is a large balcony overlooking the river. (Below) We left all the original posts and beams as well as adding a few more when the interior design required them.

FACING PAGE
Three two-sided wooden plumbing patterns form a room divider in this second-floor suite. The wall sconce, lamp and mirror are all wooden patterns. The doors to the chest are wooden patterns with metal trim. The top surface is Mexican tile. (Photo: Bluewater Photography)

The calla-lily design of one of the flour sacks found in the mill was used for our curtains and blinds. (Photo: Bluewater Photography)

FACING PAGE
Views of two of the suites in the River Mill. (Photos: Integrated Graphics)

ent problem. All the rooms but one had sliding doors on to balconies, as well as long, narrow windows. My first idea was to have something woven and very Canadian. The more I went around pricing possible fabrics, the more I realized the idea was unrealistic as I could find nothing reasonable enough to even consider.

One day, while we were cleaning out the mill before work had started, I found some old flour sacks in the basement. One of them had a lovely, simple calla-lily design with PFRIMMER, BENMILLER, ONTARIO printed on it. The design was bright red and green. With a rust-red and warm brown instead, the design would be perfect. I knew that if I used the same people who had silk-screened the material for the woollen mill, I would get the required faded look, for when I had washed some of this material which had been made into aprons, the design had all but disappeared. I asked one of the Pfrimmer brothers, a former owner of the mill, if he would mind if I used their design for our curtains, and he seemed delighted.

I bought 800 yards of old-fashioned monks' cloth, which was as close as I could get to sacking, at $1.50 per yard, loaded it into my station wagon and headed for Pickering, east of Toronto, where the silk screening was to be done. This time I chose much stronger colours than I really wanted.

Two weeks later the material was ready. When I arrived to pick it up, I asked the man to cut off a few yards. "Where is the nearest laundromat?" I asked.

When I came back I handed him the yardage to inspect. "I just don't understand it," he said in horror. "This has never happened to me before." He was greatly relieved when I told him that it was perfect. It was exactly the faded look I had hoped to achieve.

Another finishing touch was the blown-up photo of Jonathan Miller that hangs on the wall opposite the entrance. Originally I had it made for the dining room, thinking it would be a marvellous spot to display all of Jonathan's 486 pounds, but Peter thought my

*A view of a bed-
room and (inset)
a bathroom with
decorative Mexi-
can tiles. (Pho-
tos: Tom Van
Turnhout)*

*In November 1975 the River Mill opened its
doors (right) to its first guests. Above the door
can be seen the stained glass panel designed by
Peter Haworth. These handsome old doors were
from the Grand Theatre in London. Peter
designed the lamps on either side of them.*

Sitting area outside River Mill overlooking the river. (Photo: Tom Van Turnhout)

(Below) The conference room. The stone walls have been exposed. A composition of plumbing patterns decorates the walls. (Photo: Integrated Graphics)

warped sense of humour out of place in an eating area and vetoed it. He readily approved, however, of having that portly gentleman with his welcoming smile greet the guests as they entered the River Mill. Some hundred years ago, Jonathan's own hotel was directly opposite this mill. In July the tennis courts were installed, and in November 1975 the River Mill opened its doors to its first guests.

Soon work commenced on the swimming pool. This was the only time an architect was employed during the whole project. His name was Carlos Venten. Peter lacked the confidence to design a completely new building, particularly a swimming pool, which would require the technical skills of an engineer as well. It was fascinating to watch this building take shape. The men would build a complete wall out of plywood on the ground and raise it into place with long timbers. After they had finished pouring the concrete around the pool, the building seemed to go up overnight.

It was a much more "commercial-looking" building than the other two, but with the aid of such things as a circular stairway, three old church windows and a few plumbing patterns here and there, it acquired what I hoped was a Benmiller "feel."

The size and shape of the pool itself was dictated by Ontario legislation. If a pool is larger than a certain number of square feet, one has to employ a life-guard at all times. In order to make the pool as long as possible and still have enough width, we cut into one corner. This made a much larger and more interesting-looking pool and yet we still managed to comply with regulations. July of 1976, eight months after the work had begun, saw the completion of the swimming pool. The following March our pool won first

The size and shape of the pool were dictated by Ontario legislation. The whirlpool (second photo) was again the silo concept. The men (left) would build a complete wall on the ground and raise it into place with long timbers.

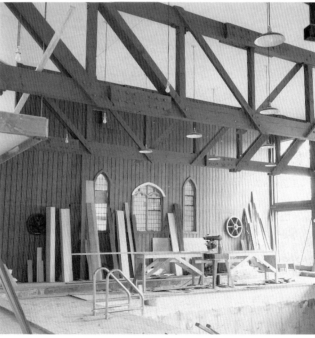

The swimming pool was a more "commercial" looking building than the other two, but with such touches as a circular staircase and three old church windows the finished result had what we hoped was the Benmiller "feel." (Photos: Cleeve Horne)

A striking view of the River Mill, where Sharpe's Creek joins the Maitland River. (Inset) The round window set in the upstream wall of the bridge offers a view of the dam. The wheel came from another old Ontario grist mill. (Photos: Integrated Graphics)

98

The swimming pool, which in March 1977 won first prize in the Design of Excellence Awards at the International Master Pool Congress in Mississippi. (Photo: Integrated Graphics)

The original kitchen went only to the corner of the old building.

prize for an indoor pool in the Design of Excellence Awards at the International Master Pool Congress in Mississippi.

Late in November 1976, just before the Christmas rush, we had another party for all those who took part in the renovation of the River Mill and construction of the swimming pool. This time we celebrated the completion of the whole Benmiller Inn complex—or so I thought.

INTO THE KITCHEN

No story of Benmiller would be complete without mentioning our problems with the kitchen.

From the outset we were ill advised. We had hired a firm in London to do the layout and supply the equipment. To save money, which at that point was disappearing at an alarming rate, we decided to go for less expensive equipment. This later turned out to be a costly mistake.

To begin with, Peter acquired, for the taking, a huge dishwasher from the cafeteria in his London plant. It was a rambling affair that took up too much precious space. He then had it completely overhauled at some expense.

By the time the chef arrived on the scene, the kitchen was nicely underway. He took one look at the layout and said it would be impossible for him to turn out a meal in such a kitchen. He insisted that it be rearranged to suit his particular talents. We soon learned that our kitchen would require a revolving stage if we were to appease each successive chef.

We had been open only a short time when the monster dishwasher broke down for good. This freed some valuable space as the more modern ones were much smaller, so with a minor shuffle we were on our way again.

From the beginning too, we had problems with the grease trap clogging up. Not only was it in the wrong place, beside the cooking range, but it was totally inadequate and had to be cleaned and treated once a month—a large job. There were complaints from the kitchen staff about the textured linoleum flooring, which was hard to keep clean. We closed down for two days and replaced it with a smooth cushioned linoleum and our next chef promptly slipped and broke his shoulder. For a month the sous chef took over. Finally, by the time the River Mill opened, we were forced to take action with the kitchen as there was insufficient space to cope with the added traffic created by the additional rooms.

While the swimming pool was under construction, Benmiller Inn closed its doors for a week to enlarge and totally remodel its kitchen. The same men worked on both construction sites and, with the help of our maintenance crew, the job was soon finished. The addition went along the north outside wall of the main building, devouring one window. On the inside in the bar area it was replaced with an antique mirror. The grease trap was moved to the basement

With the help of the maintenance staff, the men building the swimming pool remodelled the kitchen as well.

The first addition (above) went along the north wall, blocking out a window.

(Above) Back at work in the new kitchen after the first addition, before and after painting. (Photos: Tom Van Turnhout)

(Right) A few years later the kitchen was again enlarged and two more windows disappeared on the north wall.

The door to the turbine room is constructed of wooden plumbing patterns. (Photo: Bluewater Photography)

where it should have been in the first place. The new floor was tiled with non-skid tiles. We bought new equipment. Over the new cooking range went a stainless steel canopy with an exhaust fan big enough to take care of the additional space.

As usual, with solutions came new problems. The suction of the larger kitchen exhaust fan affected the air currents in the lobby and bar area, and for months we couldn't light fires in the fireplaces for fear of being smoked out. A metal cap on top of the chimney corrected the smoking, but as the mill was in a hollow, cold air was constantly sucked down the flue of the larger fireplace, making the lobby very cold in winter. Finally, an Elmira insert was put in and the problem was solved.

A few years later the kitchen was again enlarged and two more windows on the north side were gobbled up. This time we found three stained glass windows with antique mirror centres that exactly fitted the three sacrificed windows, which enhanced the bar area immeasurably. The enlarged space was created for a walk-in cooler. There was a walk-in freezer as well as a fridge in basement from the outset but it wasn't practical for the staff to constantly go down to the basement to fetch fresh vegetables, eggs and frozen meat. Hopefully the present kitchen will serve the Inn in the preparation of gourmet meals for many years to come.

HARNESSING THE ELEMENTS

Harnessing the elements for power, whether it be wind, sun or water, had always been of great interest to Peter. It had been his dream to re-activate the original power source for at least one of the mills. Though the power would have been greater in the Woollen Mill as the head of water at the upper dam was higher, the set-up for a turbine room was far better in the River Mill . Peter had been looking for someone to do the job as he himself had neither the time nor the expertise.

Harnessing the elements fascinated Peter and the turbine room was one of his favourite places. Shown here in the foreground is a 1910 Barber turbine. In the background is the electrical panel designed especially for the job by Ontario Hydro. (Photo: Bluewater Photography)

I can't remember when Peter first introduced me to Heinz Peper, but it must have been shortly after work commenced on the River Mill, for that was when Heinz's name first appeared as an expense on our monthly statement. Heinz, I think, found his way to Benmiller like a dog that smells a bitch in heat from many miles away. He must have got a whiff of our turbines and found the lure irresistible.

"What is Heinz doing here?" I asked Peter one day.

"He's re-activating the turbines so that we can use them to heat the swimming pool and hopefully the River Mill."

The old turbines were replaced by two 1910 Barber turbines that came from Meaford, Ontario, and were installed by our own maintenance crew led by Brad Vanstone. Heinz brought his own generator. He told me that he nearly lost it to the river trying to get it under the mill via the mill-race. The unit weighed about 900 pounds

The electrical panel was designed especially for the job by Ontario Hydro. The meters also came from Hydro and the switches on the panel came from the Royal York, a hotel in Toronto. The whole operation took over a year to complete. In fact, Heinz told me that, the night before the party in honour of the completion of the River Mill and pool, he had "married the meters to the switch board"—our second Benmiller wedding.

Heinz did a marvellous job, but it took a team to put the project into operation. Peter did the general layout of the room and the platform on which the equipment was installed. Heinz designed the overall concept and Bill Trick, who dealt in second-hand machinery and had bought much of the machinery taken from both mills, did the linkage between generators, exciter and governor. It was Brad's job to make sure all the necessary equipment was on the site on time and to help with its installation.

The turbine room, which is visible for all to see in the bowels of the River Mill, is like a museum with the pulleys beautifully cleaned, the machinery painted in coordinated colours and the turbines as shiny as new. It was a source of great pride to Peter. I think if anyone had asked him which room in Benmiller Inn was his favourite, he would have said, without hesitation, the turbine room.

The turbines unfortunately have not been in operation for over a year. The exciter that sets the current in motion, which came from an old navy ship, wore out and Heinz was unable to find a replacement. The present owners are hoping that someday they may be able to get a government grant to revise the system. There is adequate power potential in the lower dam to generate enough electricity to heat the River Mill as well as the swimming pool.

Through Heinz Peper, Peter acquired the whole auxiliary electrical unit from Eaton's College Street store in Toronto when the building was turned into an apartment/shopping mall complex. This equipment had never been used except for test runs yearly to make sure it was in good order. It consisted of a huge electrical panel board and three gargantuan generators each capable of generating 1000 horsepower. The equipment cost around $15,000 by the time it was delivered to Benmiller. Peter had an idea that someday it could be put into operation to supply enough power for the whole of Benmiller. An ambitious thought, and I suspect it could have been possible, but Peter went on to the next project and the generators lay outside our barn, neglected for years. The neighbours finally complained and Peter made a half-hearted attempt at selling them. Eventually he gave them away for scrap.

Adding Houses

From the beginning, Peter wanted to develop what he called Upper Lands West, the field where the barn and tennis courts are. I'm not sure how he first came in contact with Roger Hulton, whose profession it was to search out old log cabins, dismantle them, ship them and re-assemble them in new locations. Peter had decided that Upper Lands West should have old log cabins interspersed with late nineteenth-century Victorian architecture.

Our first purchase was three log houses. One was the Griffith Inn, which was remarkable because of its size. It came from Renfrew, near Ottawa. The other two were smaller cabins from northern Ontario. All the timbers were over 100 years old and in perfect condition. Upon arrival in Benmiller they were neatly laid out in numbered piles on Upper Lands West. By November 1977 architectural plans for re-assembling the Griffith Inn were put into my hands, drafted in Peter's familiar style. In order to design this house as he wanted, he had to use logs from the other two cabins.

It was a beautiful house, and no expense was spared to make it perfect. Peter had originally thought to use it as additional accommodation facilities for Benmiller Inn, until he could find a buyer who could afford it. The house was sold before it was finished.

In the summer of 1977 Peter had been told by Roger Hulton that the old Nominigan Lodge was "up for grabs." This log building in Algonquin Park had been built by the Grand Trunk Railway at the turn of the century as a fishing and hunting lodge. The park authorities were tearing down many of the buildings in the Park and the lodge was next on the list. It was ours for a relatively small price if we wanted to dis-

Log house under construction using timbers from the Griffith Inn.

Preceding page
This rose-coloured stained glass window was originally above the door leading to the balcony over the lower pond, forming an atrium in the Gledhill House. Because of the change in fire regulations, the ceiling had to be lowered, creating an extra room above. This window and a skylight above it are now part of that room.

In September 1977 we bought the old Gledhill House built in 1906. It was in a lovely setting overlooking the lower pond. (Photos: Ray Anabe)

mantle it and haul it away. It had been a marvellous building of its kind in Algonquin Park, but no matter how hard I tried I couldn't see it fitting into the Benmiller complex. Peter wanted to erect it on Upper Lands West, just above the Woollen Mill, and use it for extra units.

Peter was soon busy drawing up plans to submit to the authorities. He was hoping that we might get government help under the label of a "heritage project," but I wasn't sure that I wanted the building even if it cost us nothing. Peter had to alter the original building to such a degree to suit our needs that the government wasn't interested. It would have cost us well over a million dollars to construct it as Peter had designed it. I dug in my heels, secretly relieved that we couldn't get assistance.

The fact remained that we still needed more sleeping space and conference space to make Benmiller viable. Long gone was our original idea of a little wayside inn with a few rooms. Even after the River Mill opened we knew that more space was needed.

That November we purchased the old Gledhill House and the Gledhills moved to Goderich. Peter had an idea of using the house for staff accommodation. The current manager had always had grave doubts about the Nominigan Lodge, not only because of its appearance but because of its proposed location. When we discussed the alternatives, the Gledhill seemed the obvious choice as an annex.

The construction of the house was concrete brick and it was built in 1906. Ward and his family lived there until Ward's death in 1943, when Verne and Willa moved in with Clyde. We took possession of the Gledhill House in September of 1977. This is part of a letter written by Peter to Verne around that time:

Since our first real estate transaction seven years ago much water has flowed down Sharpe's Creek and under the bridge. Despite some disappointing periods in that time for us, one of the most pleasant things about it all has been our association with both of you. When you move, you won't be that far away and we'll ensure that that association continues.

The house was halfway between the Woollen and the River Mills in a lovely setting overlooking the lower pond. There was enough land around it for parking and an extension to include the required seventeen units. Using the Miller's House would be consistent with the Benmiller theme.

Peter had just recovered from a nasty session with the flu. In the middle of March he took off for three weeks in the Virgin Islands, but before he left we had a serious discussion about the idea of using the Gledhill House. He was still feeling very weak.

"I'm tired," he said. "If that's what you want, you do it yourself."

There is a wonderful old manor house well back off Highway 8 on the Maitland River close to Goderich. It had always intrigued me and I thought a similar treatment of the Gledhill House might work well: that is, using the house as the centre of the building, with wings on either side.

I took pictures of the manor house and presented them to Peter when he arrived home in early April. He was feeling much stronger after his holiday and, as I expected, immediately became interested. We hired Ray Anabe, who had worked with the architect on the swimming pool, to draw up the plans to Peter's specifications, and we were off again.

At the beginning we worked fairly closely together on the plans. Then Peter sprang the ugly question, "How are we going to pay for this new building?" When the estimates started to come in it was obvious that the job was going to take some heavy financing, and we would both have to put in a large chunk of it ourselves. Peter and I were a partnership from the beginning. That is, we always had equal equity in the whole project, but it had long worried me that I had little control over the purse strings. Peter had an office and secretary at his disposal, as well as years of business experience, so it was natural that he would attend to all business details.

"It would only further confuse the managerial staff if there were two bosses to answer to," he said. So I tried to stay clear of that department. The same could be said of the construction crew as well.

The larger our complex grew, however, the more difficult it became for me. I kept hearing my late father's voice over my shoulder: "Get out, Joanne.

The pond was emptied and banks were shored up ready for the foundation before the go-ahead for work on the Gledhill House was received.

Footings were laid for the long wings, which were angled so as to diminish the impression of length, and forms were built for the poured concrete foundation. (Photos: Ray Anabe)

The foundation takes shape. (Upper photos: Ray Anabe)

The exterior walls were cement block to blend with the old house.

The mansard roof with gables on the second floor.

The building was covered with an antique white plaster, and finally the black shingles went on the mansard roof.

110

Enough is enough." He had always worried about my involvement in Benmiller.

I was finally ready to listen, for I realized that being in partnership with Peter was a luxury I could no longer afford. Peter had come into possession of Cherrydale Farm in February of 1976 and had been trying to sell it ever since. I had lived in the farmhouse in the summer of 1977 while I was building my own house nearby and had fallen in love with it.

We had been trying to figure out how we could dissolve the partnership fairly when I told Peter that I would take Cherrydale and the surrounding land as part of the deal. He was only too glad to get rid of it, and only too glad for it to fall into the hands of his sister so that Benmiller would still have free access to the ski trails. This being settled, Peter said that he hoped I would remain involved long enough to do the interior of Gledhill House.

"What payment would you want?" he asked.

"Nothing," I said. "I would be delighted to do it, but no surprises." I remembered in the early days when we had first started work on the Woollen Mill, Peter arrived back from a trip to Hong Kong with two dozen beautiful, large Chinese lamps, complete with shades. I said no, for I couldn't envisage Chinese lamps as fitting decor for our project. In April of 1978 we dissolved our partnership of eight years.

THE GLEDHILL HOUSE

As soon as the plans for the Gledhill House were completed, we submitted them to the authorities for approval. We planned to use the old house in its entirety. We would build large wings out on either side with gables on the second floor and a mansard roof as in the manor house I had seen on Highway 8. We would angle the wings in such a way as to diminish the long appearance of the building. We had hired Fred Fones, the same contractor from London who had worked with such success on the River Mill and the swimming pool, and were ready to go.

The old staircase in the Gledhill House was retained. (Photo: Bluewater Photography)

111

As we had run out of wrought iron logos, Peter had the design copied in aluminium. When it was painted black, you couldn't tell the difference. Each balcony and all the bedheads were decorated with these pieces. (Photo: Bluewater Photography)

This concave cast iron grille forms part of a room divider in the lobby. Originally it was placed on top of the dye vats in the woollen mill to hold the wool being dyed. (Photo: Bluewater Photography)

FACING PAGE
Room 70, which at one time was the upper part of the atrium beneath. (Photo courtesy of Benmiller Inn)

The lamps as usual were "works of Art." Some were made from posts of old staircases. The leaf design was snipped off the top of an old wire fence. The parchment shades decorated with dried flowers were executed by Betty McKnight. The little lamp was a spool from the Woollen Mill. (Photos: Bluewater Photography)

(Below) Barley put into wet plaster decorates the wall sconces in the hallways and as an accent by the doors into each bedroom. (Photo: Bluewater Photography)

Months passed with no word of approval from the authorities. There had been a misunderstanding between the Ministry of Housing and the County Planning Department, and the local council refused to issue us a building permit. We were in a panic of frustration, for we knew that if the footings for the wings were not poured before winter set in, it would be a very costly delay of a good six months or more. The banks of the pond had already been shored up in hope that permission to proceed would come at any time. Finally in desperation we went ahead with the footings and held our breath.

At last, in late December, we were issued a building permit. The misunderstanding had developed when the Ministry of Housing refused permission to build the added units because it conflicted with the township's secondary plan. The County Planning Board had given its approval because it conformed with the plan. Council couldn't decide who was right. It turned out that the Ministry had based its decision on the wrong plan. There was also concern over whether there would be adequate parking space for guests. This was sparked by the workers leaving their vehicles all over the county road adjacent to the site, making passage around the parked cars difficult for the residents. This problem too was eventually solved, and once permission to proceed was granted, the building progressed quickly.

By that summer we were well on our way. There were many "surprises" in store before the Gledhill was completed. In fact, Peter was really largely responsible for most of the interior and exterior details of that building.

Ever since the opening of the River Mill, the Lieutenant Governor at that time, the Honourable Pauline McGibbon, and her husband, Don, had spent a few days with us each summer. That July, when they were staying at Benmiller, I asked them if they would like to see through the new building. I remember the roof was just going into place and Her Honour was gin-

View of the Gledhill House in spring from across the pond. The second photo shows the solar panels on the roof.

The original tin dining and living room ceilings were maintained. (Photo: Tom Van Turnhout)

gerly picking her way through the loose timbers. As we passed some of the workmen I heard one say to the other in a very loud whisper, "Hey, do you see who that is? That's Pauline. You know the Lieutenant Governor."

Her Honour stopped in her tracks. I held my breath for I didn't know what to do or say. She turned around and with her wonderful, warm smile she put out her hand to the man who had been speaking. He hesitantly took it and then practically shook it off.

"I just want to tell you," she said, "that you boys are doing the most marvellous job. The place is simply beautiful," and with that she walked on.

The next day, when I went in to check on things, the same workman came up to me. He put out his hand and said to me, "You see this hand. Pauline touched it. As I said to the missus, it'll never get washed again."

For some time Aunt Betty had been working hard on the dried flower pictures which hang on the walls in each of the rooms. By the time she had finished, she had done fifty in all. The tiles with the numbers on the doors and the birds in the bathrooms were hand painted by Herta Sand, a friend of our first manager, in Toronto. I had used them in Cherrydale Farm and Peter like them so much he ordered them for the Gledhill House.

It was Peter's idea to put the barley in the plaster around the doors and I had suggested that we do the same thing around the wall sconces. He loved the original old tin ceilings in what had been the dining and living rooms, so he insisted that they be saved. They add a great deal to the two bedrooms on the ground floor of the centre part of the house.

As we had run out of "logo" wrought iron for the bedheads, Peter had it copied in aluminium, and when it was painted you couldn't tell the difference unless, of course, you happened to lift it. The lamps again were mostly "works of Art."

The large pine mirrors were bought from an an-

The Gledhill demonstrated Peter's usual attention to detail. Shown here are balconies, with our logo, the door into the right wing, and a downpipe and eavestrough.

Gledhill House in the fall. The bank surrounding the lower pond is always a blaze of colour at this time of year. (Right) The lower atrium with its recycled doors and windows.

tique dealer near Elmira. I picked up the first dozen in my station wagon on a blustery winter's day. The driving conditions were about as bad as they could get, with icy roads and blowing snow creating such white-outs that they reduced visibility to zero. I made my way carefully along Highway 8, and when I reached one of the last curves in the road before the Benmiller turn-off, my back tire caught the lip at the edge of the pavement and the car spun into the path of an oncoming huge transport trailer. There was no way he could slow down and there was nothing I could do except turn the wheels instinctively in the opposite direction and pray.

I can remember saying to myself, "O dear God, not yet. I still have too much to do." Then my wheels found a large bare section of the road and just before we were about to collide, my car followed the direction of the wheels and went careening back across the road and down into a deep snow bank. My car was completely immersed in the snow. For a moment I didn't move. When I was sure I was all right, I looked around to check the mirrors. They hadn't even budged. The car had been cushioned by the snow. Shaken but unharmed, I lowered my window and started to dig myself into view. A kind passing motorist went to the nearest garage for help, and soon I was hauled out of the bank and on my way with not a scratch to show for my narrow escape.

The solar heating system of the Gledhill was another of Peter's pet projects. The concept fascinated him. The building is heated by heat pumps that collect and concentrate the BTUs stored in a large thermal tank in the basement of the old section of the building. The tank has a capacity of about 20,000 gallons of water and is fuelled by solar panels on the roof of the original house. The water in the tank stores temperatures up to 92°F. In the summer the Gledhill House is cooled by water from Sharpe's Creek.

The storage tank is one of three iron tanks that Peter salvaged from an oil company. Another of those

Willa Gledhill in front of the house during construction.

The Pfrimmer house (now Mill House) before we purchased it in 1971. The photo below shows the house after renovation began in the summer of 1973.

For a few years Mill House was the manager's house. In the early 1980s it was expanded to make two suites and two more bedrooms. (Photo: Tom Van Turnhout)

Inside one of the suites at Mill House.
(Photo courtesy of Benmiller Inn)

tanks, with both ends cut off, serves as a bridge across the creek on the ski trail below Cherrydale Farm. The last one is buried under my house at Benmiller in case I should decide at a later date to solar heat my house as well. Solar heating has worked well in the Gledhill House. The cost of heating this building is a fraction of what it costs to heat the two mills.

The Gledhill quietly opened its doors in April of 1979. An early guest to stay in the building was Willa Gledhill, the former owner. Verne had died the year before. This is part of the letter I received from Willa, dated December 2, 1979.

Dear Joanne:

Just a short note to thank you for our lovely visit at the Gledhill House. My niece Marion came along with me and we both enjoyed it very much. I even had my old bedroom and they had the bed in the right place, too. Everything is so beautiful that it made me feel good. I can say it did bring back memories and they were all good ones—I am only sorry that he (Verne) couldn't have lived long enough to see the house as it is now. He was so interested in it, but didn't even get out very often to see what they were doing. He always said it will be beautiful when Peter and Joanne are doing it. He had the greatest regard for both of you, said so many times that it was good for the Mill, our house, in fact for all Benmiller that you came to Benmiller.

It meant much to Peter and me to have the approval of the Gledhills and I shall always cherish that letter.

Next came the purchase of the house between the Gledhill House and Woollen Mill. Verne Gledhill had lived in it before moving to the Gledhill House. It became a new manager's house, freeing Mill House near the River Mill to become four more suites. Peter's daughter Barbara re-did the interior of Mill House and it is utterly charming. The treatment is again entirely different. She used chintz and soft colours totally in keeping with the ambience of the house with its lovely view of the river.

Cherrydale

"CHERRY DALE FARM", RES. OF J.C. LE TOUZEL, CON.1. LOT 6, COLBORNE TP. ONT.

Etching of Cherrydale Farm from the old Huron County Atlas of 1871.

THE LAST BUILDING that Benmiller took over was my Cherrydale Farm. Though I owned it, Peter suggested that it might be better for both of us if the Inn rented it from me to operate as extra sleeping space. After I had acquired the farm from Peter, I had renovated and furnished it and from July 1979 to May 1983 I operated it as a guest farm. I was relieved to have Benmiller rent it, for it had never been profitable for me because of the number of staff I had to hire.

Cherrydale was the first farm house in Colborne Township. Michael Fisher had purchased 5,465 acres from the Canada Company in 1829 and in 1834 built a large stone dwelling on this land. As in most stone houses of this period, the walls were constructed two and a half feet thick and the stone was faced with roughcast. The framing was of oak timbers, and the house was built on two levels. The main level was three storeys high. The lower level was one large room, and in it was a huge fireplace with a baking oven attached. This room was originally the kitchen, but later became a blacksmith's shop where the horses were led through an oversized door in the lower level at the back, to be shod. This same door now welcomes cross-country skiers to come in to warm themselves before the same large fireplace, and to partake of hot cider and soup.

There was a sawmill and a small furniture factory on the property, which Fisher had already con-structed to help with the building of the house. The sawmill was down by the river and powered by a creek. The remains of the old dam that created a head of eight feet can still be seen today. The big cedar swamp up the creek from Cherrydale was the source of the Fisher Creek, but as land was sold, cleared and drained the creek all but disappeared. Some years ago the dam was rebuilt with the idea of making a trout pond, but, because of the fast flow from the melting snow during the spring season, it was soon washed away.

Michael Fisher was forced to sell off a greater portion of his land to pay for the house. The following excerpt from a report on "Huron County and the Affairs of the Canada Company," sent to the Legislative Assembly of Upper Canada, explains some of the problems the early settlers ran into with the company:

"Mr. Michael Fisher, a highly respectable settler in the Township of Colborne—the possessor and occupier of upwards of 5,000 acres of land, all paid for, the owner of a large and thriving stock and a sawmill and having upwards of 120 acres cleared—applied to the Commissioners of the Canada Company two or three years ago for a loan to enable him to build a substantial Stone House for the better accommodation of his numerous and rising family. This worthy and industrious man who abandoned a noble farm in Yonge St. failed in his attempt to raise a loan in any other quarter and was compelled by his necessities to sell 600 or

Aerial view of Cherrydale Farm, showing the addition to the left of the building. The etching from the Huron County Atlas was rendered from the far side of the house.

700 acres of his choicest land. Mr. Commissioner Alan of the Canada Company became the purchaser. The Company's price at that time was £12 1/6d [or $15 per acre]. The price given to Mr. Fisher was £7 1/6d—the price he had paid several years before."

Michael Fisher still had sufficient holdings to give each of his seven sons 300 acres before he left in 1844. At this time he traded his farm and two others to J.H. Martin for a chopping mill, flour mill, saw mill and forty acres back in York County. In 1874 Martin sold the house and 150 acres to James Le Touzel. It was Le Touzel who named the farm Cherrydale because of its large cherry orchard. Since that time unfortunately, the trees have been left to grow wild and many have been chopped down.

Later Le Touzel was to build, down the slope behind the house near the creek, a large building where he brewed and bottled what he called cham-

pagne, using fresh cold water from the fast-flowing creek and grapes grown on his farm. He delivered the brew himself to the many hotels and grog shops in the surrounding villages. He also grew sorghum, from which he made a syrup that was used on bread or pancakes. Sorghum is a tall grass grown for its edible seed and sweet juice. The stalks are put through a roller machine and the juice is boiled into syrup.

In the early 1880s Le Touzel sold Cherrydale to John Rossier, who was partially crippled. He had never married so employed James White and his wife to manage the farm for him. After his death, the Whites acquired Cherrydale, and then their daughter

The remains of the old dam that created a head of eight feet can still be seen.

and her husband after them until in 1918 it was sold to John Durst. In 1921 Durst sold it to Tobias Fisher, a descendant of Michael Fisher, who lived in it for thirteen years, when it was returned to John Durst. For nine years Cherrydale remained empty as John Durst and his family lived on a farm on the Holmesville road nearby. In 1940 the family moved to Cherrydale and lived there until John died in 1954. His son Albert and family stayed on to operate Cherrydale as a guest farm until 1975, when he sold it.

The new owner came to my brother to see if he would finance him. He wanted to have a herb farm along with raising cattle. In February of 1976 Peter was forced to foreclose as the owner was unable to meet his commitment and had run heavily into debt. Peter immediately put it on the market and I hoped and prayed that no one would buy it. I knew what a beautiful property it was as our Benmiller trails ran across it. When Peter and I dissolved our partnership in March of 1978, I was only too glad to acquire it as part of the deal.

My restoration of Cherrydale was not an extensive one as Albert Durst and his wife, Phyllis, had renovated it a few years before. Albert was a carpenter and he and his three sons had done the work themselves.

Many years before, the kitchen had been moved from the lower area to the main floor where the living room is now. It was John Durst, Albert's father, who extended the house beyond the verandah in the front to make a new kitchen and, above, bathrooms. He also closed in the remaining part of the verandah. Albert and Phyllis completely remodelled the kitchen, built the fireplace in the living room and lowered the ceiling. Phyllis was a marvellous cook and frequently prepared as many as fifty meals at a time in her well-organized kitchen.

Because I had camped in Cherrydale for the summer months two years before I acquired it, I knew what would have to be done to make it more comfortable without sacrificing sleeping space. The first thing

126

It was a labour of love to revitalize this beautiful old farmhouse.

John Durst and his wife in front of Cherry-dale Farm before they renovated it around 1940. It was John Durst who filled in the verandah and extended the house in front to make a kitchen and, above it, a bathroom. (Photos courtesy of Norman Durst)

I did was to hire Albert Durst and his three sons to do the renovation, as I felt they would know better than anyone what lay behind each wall.

The windows were the first thing to be replaced as they were over 100 years old (Albert thought they were probably the original ones). The heat had inadvertently been left off without draining the system the first winter Peter owned it so most of the pipes had to be replaced. I exposed the old stone walls on the inside wherever possible and squeezed in two more bathrooms, one off the bedroom on the main floor and one in the attic, which I had converted into a sleeping space. The only extension that was built that year was to fill in the space under the bedroom over the front door to create an office and a front vestibule. Albert had opened this area up some years before when he took the farm over. The new verandah around Cherrydale was built to appease the fire department. They decided that Cherrydale should be treated as a hotel and therefore would need an exit on both sides of the house on the main and second floors (the third floor was treated as a loft to the room below). Rather than hack through the two-and-a-half-foot stone wall, I designed a verandah to extend along three sides of the house, which then gave an exit from each room while improving its overall appearance.

It wasn't until the following year that I extended the Forge below, creating a terrace and screened-in porch above. At the same time the stone was removed from the back of the large fireplace and fireproof glass was put in its place so that the fire could be viewed, if not felt, from both sides. Finally, two years later, as the roughcast was crumbling from the exterior of the building, I had it removed and the old stone sandblasted and pointed. It was a labour of love to revitalize that beautiful old farmhouse.

In May of 1995 Cherrydale again became a private residence and it is no longer part of the Benmiller Inn complex.

Cherrydale before the verandah was added.

The space under the bedroom by the front entrance was filled in to make an office.

(Top) The back of the house before the Forge was extended. The new verandah (above) was built to appease the fire department. It extended along three sides of the house, creating a fire exit for each bedroom. (Right) View from the screened porch of the new addition.

The Forge was originally a kitchen, then a blacksmith's shop. The original mantel on the large fireplace was replaced in 1986 with a hand-hewn beam from an old log cabin. The stone wall was removed from the back of the fireplace (below) and replaced with fireproof glass so that the fire could be seen from both sides. Shown above are plough seats at the counter in the Forge.

The attic was converted into an extra sleeping space with four beds and a bathroom. (Photos: Bluewater Photography)

Looking Back

IN FEBRUARY of 1984 Benmiller Inn was sold. Peter had died the year before and there was no one in his family or mine who wished to become an innkeeper.

For many years now, friends have wondered how I can remain in the village of Benmiller and watch Peter's and my child being cared for by someone else. It is surprising how detached one can become. I suppose if the child were being mistreated I would feel differently, but whenever I visit the Inn I am delighted at how healthy and contented it looks. Aged a little, a few wrinkles here and there, but that is to be expected, for it was well aged to begin with.

Peter and I were both great scroungers. All the secondhand junk dealers in southern Ontario knew us well. We both felt that old materials should be used wherever possible to give the Inn an authentic appearance. The large handsome doors to the private dining room and the entrance doors to the River Mill were from the Grand Theatre in London. The steel girders holding up both mills and the swimming pool were part of the old bridge across the Maitland River. The church windows on the end wall of the swimming pool came from a church on Yonge Street in Toronto that had been destroyed by fire. The large stone carving inside the entrance gates to the Woollen Mill was part of the façade of the old Customs House that our wrought iron logo came from. The front door to the Gledhill House came from an old

mansion in Toronto. The door is two inches thick and is one piece of wood with a beautiful panel of bevelled glass. The doors and windows in the atrium of the Gledhill were bought from a store in Toronto that deals in nothing but antique doors and windows. The list is endless. Using the old has played a large part in the overall flavour of antiquity we tried to achieve.

Benmiller was conceived as an adult oasis. As such hospitality is of paramount importance. Peter and I soon discovered that in the running of a country inn, no matter how attractive the place is physically, it is the staff from the kitchen to the front desk that are responsible for making a four-star establishment. The friendliness of the staff, their attentiveness and efficiency, the food and the general upkeep of the whole complex are the ingredients necessary to make sure that the same guests return time and time again. This is what earned us in December of 1985 the prestigious Andrew Harper's Hideaway Report Award for the best Country House Hotel of the year. This is a worldwide award and we were the second Canadian hotel ever to achieve this distinction.

From the beginning I kept a fairly complete pictorial record of the renovation and construction of both mills, the pool and the Gledhill House. This was fortunate, for whenever my memory fails me, one glance through my albums and the image comes back into focus. Every time I go through the exercise I marvel anew at Peter's expertise in so many areas. To watch him in action on the Benmiller site was a revelation. He was fascinated with the unknown and untried. Whenever something new appeared on the market he had to try it out. He was ahead of his time in so many ways. His background in the plumbing and heating business served him well, but there was more to it than that—it was his fine taste and integrity that helped give Benmiller the "class" and individuality it possesses.

We were both self-taught in architecture, design and the ways of the hospitality business. The lessons we learned were often a gruelling test to our endurance and fortitude, but when I look back on it all I can truthfully say, "Yes, it was worth it."

The one thing that has never changed in Benmiller is its timeless beauty.

Some comments in the press...

London Free Press, summer 1974: Saul Holiff

"Nestled in the Maitland Valley, in the rustic, undulating countryside of Huron County, Benmiller is a place of unexpected beauty.... The old former Gledhill woollen mill on Sharpe's Creek, once famous for its Benmiller blankets, recently has been imaginatively restored and turned into an elegant country inn nonpareil."

London Free Press, Travel Section, February 1975: Betty Smith

"Every now and then we look for that special place to add to our scrapbook of memories for our old age. So far this winter we have discovered one close to home.... If you are looking for perfection at the end of a day's skiing or just walking in the beauty and peace of Huron county, it is to be found at the Mill in Benmiller, near Goderich."

Detroit News, December 1975

"Nestled in the rolling landscape along a wide placidly winding river is the hamlet of Benmiller where a unique country inn has emerged in the last year and a half.... One can imagine how spectacular it must be in a fresh snowfall or surrounded by the profusion of bright summer flowers which grow all around it but somehow the sombre grays and browns of an early winter landscape suit it well.... For city dwellers who long to escape occasionally to a truly unspoiled country setting this restoration has done a brilliant service."

Dining Out with Tom Kelly, London News, November 3, 1976

"The Benmiller is one of the most respected inns in Canada."

Toronto Life, January 1977

"Benmiller Inn – just about the most comfortable and relaxing place imaginable."

Grosse Pointe War Memorial Association, May 1977

"One of Canada's most deluxe and original hostelries – a unique showplace."

Detroit Free Press, Travel Resorts, August 28, 1977: George Cantor

"It is this concern with the integrity of the past amid all the comforts of the present that gives the inn its unique spirit."

Long Beach Independent Press Telegram, California, October 9, 1977: Herb Shannon

"The result is a luxurious rural retreat on 75 acres of glorious wooded wonderland."

Selling Travel magazine, November 15, 1977

"Set in a secluded valley near Goderich, Ontario is a complex of strikingly renovated century old mills offering a luxurious resort with modern comforts and country charm."

***Michigan Living Motor News*, May 1978: Len Barnes**

"'Undiscovered Gem' is a term no travel writer should toss around lightly. I've used it fewer than six times in 32 years of describing resorts, tourist areas and restaurants in 52 countries I've visited but it fits a place only a couple of hours' drive into Ontario from Detroit. The Benmiller Inn, three miles outside Goderich and 77 miles from Port Huron's Blue Water Bridge, is truly an undiscovered gem."

***Globe and Mail*, Travel Section, August 5, 1978**

"Two nineteenth century mills, one a former grist mill and the other a woollen mill, combine to make this a luxurious hideaway in the pretty Maitland Valley."

***Sunday Sun*, Toronto, January 21, 1979: Bev Spencer**

"Attention to detail is the factor that separates a good inn from an outstanding one.... There are the small touches that set Benmiller apart as something special.... The main dining area overlooks the rushing waters of a stream. It is there that you feel closest to the history of the inn.... In keeping with the rest of the inn, the cuisine at Benmiller is superior."

***Gourmet Magazine*, August 1979**

"It's the kind of refuge travellers dream of finding at the end of a long and weary road: rustic and quiet, yet luxurious; secluded but easily accessible; and simple, in a stylish sort of way. There are forty-two comfortable and attractive rooms, none of which are alike, but all bear the stamp of a well defined taste."

Centrefold of Air Canada *En Route* magazine, March 1980

"With the wave of a wand... a pioneer village was created.... On a crisp quiet summer night you can barely hear the constant, timeless flow of water and you get a sense, for a moment at least, of the presence of the past without having to give up one little bit of modern-day comfort."

***The Hide-Away Report – A Connoisseur's Guide to Peaceful and Unspoiled Places* (a worldwide report), June 1982**

"The delightful restoration succeeded by blending contemporary creative comforts with historic authenticity – the distinct character and architectural lines of the old buildings being completely retained.... The feeling of well-being here is unassailable."

***LeisureWays*, CAA magazine, November 1986**

"Benmiller Inn... is an imaginative study in country restoration.... Through the course of nine years... they have just about restored the old town of Benmiller. Staying at Benmiller Inn is like visiting an old English country manor village.... The touches in restoration and decor alone make Benmiller a fascinating place."

***Sunday Sun*, July 1980**

"The atmosphere is one of splendid isolation."